EMANCIPATION PROCLAMATION
THE TRUE BLACK HISTORY

The journey from the valley of darkness by African slaves in 1619, to the mountain top in 2008 with the election of African American Barak Obama, President of the United States

JAMES C. ROLLINS

outskirts
press

Outskirts Press, Inc.
http://www.outskirtspress.com

ISBN: 978-1-9772-1230-6

Outskirts Press and the "OP" logo are trademarks belonging to Outskirts Press, Inc.

PRINTED IN THE UNITED STATES OF AMERICA

Acknowledgment

At (77 yrs old), this book is my heartfelt obligation to ensure that my (six) grandchildren and (three) great grandchildren- all loves of my life- have a clear understanding of their history. I also hope that they share that knowledge with other Black kids as they grow.

Thanks also to R. Edward Kennedy and Willamina Samuels for their patience and support.

INTRODUCTION

True black history has been benchmarked by a series of social engineering events designed to diminish or destroy African American society. We are today, the product of political, social, and legal events at every milestone that African Americans have passed in which something would occur that was either disruptive or destructive.

Life under slavery was awful; Emancipation was supposed to eliminate those conditions. Emancipation gifted newly freed slaves with, the re-birth of white supremacy in the South which was accompanied by Black Codes, Chain Gangs, Peonage, Convict Leasing, and finally the Ku Klux Klan. In 1865 and 1866, state governments in the South enacted laws designed to regulate the lives of the former slaves. Between the years 1889 through 1918, at least 3,224 people were lynched in America of that number 2,522 were black.

Out-migration from slavery should have been the beginning of a dream based on the initial success of Black Wall Street. Black Wall Street should have been used as the shining example going forward because it represented what Black community building success should look like. That dreamed died, and it was never to be realized again.

Cabrini Greene, the end of the migration dream, represented the devastating effects of racial, social engineering through the introduction of Super Blocks. Segregation released the creative spirits of those who would oppress and dominate the weak and defenseless. Thus Cabrini Greene.

Table of Contents

CHAPTER 1

PLANTATION SOCIAL DEVELOPMENT

Slave Introduction To America

African Americans searching for the African roots of their culture should begin by understanding that only about five percent of between 11 and 12 million enslaved Africans were brought to North America or the United States. Approximately 95 percent of the people exported from Africa were sold to "tropical America," the Caribbean basin. Most of these transported Africans were taken from West and West-Central Africa. The majority, perhaps more than 40 percent, came from West-Central Africa, the Congo-Angola region now known as contemporary Angola and the Republic of the Congo. As much as 33 percent of the slave population came from West Africa. The majority of the ancestors of African Americans, it seems, came from a part of Africa bounded by the river Senegal in the North and by Angola in the South.

By 1619 the first African indentured servants arrived in the American colonies. The indentured servant was not a slave; they were under contract to provide service, over some time, after which they were set free. This explained free Blacks in the northern states while slavery existed in the south at the same time.

The first slaves were brought into New Amsterdam (later, New York City). By 1690, every colony had slaves. In 1712 a letter purported to be a verbatim account of a short speech given by a slave owner, Willie Lynch, in which he tells other slave masters that he has discovered the "secret" to controlling black slaves by setting them against one another.

The slaves were revolting, and the plantation owners were slaughtered while they slept. Social engineers introduced the solutions, Willie Lynch, taught them the art of fear and love to manage their slaves. Punish the male in public and teach the women to" love and trust only their master and their family" and they will teach their children. The effects will last for generations.

Creoles, the First African Americans, and Creolization

In North America, the African population that came over as slaves had begun to reproduce itself by the 1730s. Before the 1730s, the Black people had to be continuously replenished by the slave trade, because most Blacks either died without reproducing or died before reaching adulthood. During the 1730s this changed and what emerged was a locally-born African-American population that we call Creole Blacks. These Creole Blacks were the first African Americans, and their process of bridging African and American worlds is what we refer to as creolization.

African-Americans Creoles, born after the 1730s, were unlike their ancestors in many respects because they were born in America. By about 1820, almost 90 percent of Black American slaves were American-born. We must, therefore, distinguish the African-born population, which became quite negligible by 1800, and the American-born Creole population that became dominant after 1820, because African-American culture begins with this Creole population.

The cultural presence of native Africans in America, was fragile because, from the eighteenth century, the African population becomes a Creole population, a homegrown population whose linkage and ties to Africa became less and less intense. Early in the nineteenth century, that balance was 51 percent women, 49 percent of men constituted an excellent ratio for sustaining population growth.

In creating their culture, the Creole population built upon what they knew of the culture of their fathers and mothers. Moreover, out of this process, this creolization and adaptation to a new environment would emerge and remain very much alive in certain cultural principles, such as religious ideas, worldviews, family structure, ways of socializing children, methods of cooking food, and so on. In other words, although this Creole population had become dominant, it was not an entirely Europeanized or Americanized population. It drew upon African cultural strengths, manifested in funeral ceremonies, burial rites, the naming of children, beliefs in amulets, charms, hags, and witches. Even the Muslim presence survived. The African roots of African-American culture lie, therefore, in a variety of dynamic cultural principles that the first Black Creole population blended and reshaped into the cultural beliefs and precepts of their American environment. Black dance movements, the spirituals, the blues, and eventually jazz are probably products of creolization and adaptation to a new environment. The current Black Islamic movement is perhaps a creolization of imported Muslim principles

Historical Significance of the Cotton Gin

In 1793 the cotton gin made the cotton industry of the south explode. Before its invention, separating cotton fibers from its seeds was a labor-intensive and unprofitable venture. After Eli Whitney unveiled his cotton gin, processing cotton became much easier, resulting in greater availability and cheaper cotton cloth. The invention also had the harmful by-product of increasing the number of slaves needed to pick the cotton and thereby strengthening the arguments for continuing slavery. Cotton as a cash crop became so vital that it was known as King Cotton and affected politics up until the Civil War.

The Underground Railroad

Between 1831 – 1861 approximately 75,000 slaves escape to the North using the Underground Railroad.

The Underground Railroad, was a network of people, both African American as well as white that provided aid to escaped slaves from the South. It operated between 1831 – 1861 approximately 75,000 slaves escape to the North using the Underground Railroad to enlist in the army to fight in the Civil War.

Quaker Abolitionists

The Quakers and the African Methodist were considered the first organized groups to actively help escaped slaves. Quaker abolitionist Isaac T. Hopper set up a network in Philadelphia. Simultaneously, in the early 1800s the African Methodist Episcopal Church, established in 1816, was another proactive religious group helping fugitive slaves.

What Was the Underground Railroad?

The term Underground Railroad came in to use after 1831 runaway slave Tice Davids escaped from Kentucky to Ohio, and his owner blamed an underground railroad for helping Davids to freedom.

In 1839, a Washington newspaper reported an escaped slave named Jim had revealed his plan to escape north following an "underground railroad to Boston." At that point, the term Underground Railroad was part of the runaway slave vernacular by 1840. "Conductors" were the people that guided most slaves helped by the Underground Railroad until they got to certain points beyond the Border States farther north.

> *"I was free, but there was no one to welcome me to the land of freedom. I was a stranger in a strange land."*
> — Attributed to Harriet Tubman

Harriet Tubman, the most famous conductor for the Underground Railroad, was born a slave named Araminta Ross; she took the name Harriet Tubman when she married. She escaped a plantation in Maryland with two of her brothers in 1849 where she ultimately made her way to Pennsylvania.

Harriet later returned to the plantation on several occasions to rescue family members and others. On her third trip, she tried to rescue her husband, but he had remarried and refused to leave.

Distraught, Tubman reported a vision of God that guided her to joined the Underground Railroad and began guiding other escaped slaves. She regularly took groups of escapees to Canada using hiding places in private homes, churches, and school houses that were part of the network. These places were called "stations," safe houses, and depots." The people operating them were called "stationmasters."

Fugitive Slave Acts

Many escapees headed for Canada because of the Fugitive Slave Acts t, passed in 1793, allowed local governments to apprehend and deport escaped slaves from within the borders of Free states back to their point of origin while punishing anyone who helped the fugitive slaves. Some Northern states tried to combat this with the ill-fated Personal Liberty Laws, which were struck down by the Supreme Court in 1842. The Fugitive Slave Act of 1850 strengthened the previous law, and this update created harsher penalties that promoted favoritism towards slave owners and led to some freed slaves being recaptured. Consequently, an escaped slave concluded that northern states were still considered a risk.

Canada offered blacks the freedom to live where they wanted, sit on juries, run for public office and more, and efforts at extradition had largely failed. Some Underground Railroad operators based themselves in Canada working to help the arriving ex-slaves settle in.

1860 Abraham Lincoln was elected president, angering the southern states, ultimately leading to 1861 when the Civil War begins.

In1863 Abraham Lincoln's Emancipation Proclamation proclaims that all slaves in rebellious territories are forever free.

Emancipation

President Abraham Lincoln did not make the abolition of slavery a goal of the Union war effort at the outset of the Civil War. He feared it would drive the border slave states still loyal to the Union into the Confederacy. By the summer of 1862, the slaves themselves had pushed the issue, heading by the thousands to the Union lines as Lincoln's troops marched through the South. Their actions debunked one of the myths that many slaves were truly content in bondage, convincing Lincoln that emancipation had become a political and military neces-sity. Lincoln's Emancipation Proclamation freed more than 3 million slaves in the Confederate states by January 1, 1863, blacks enlisted in the Union Army in large numbers, reaching some 180,000 by war's end.

During Reconstruction, the Republican Party in the South represented a coalition of blacks made up the overwhelming majority of Republican voters in the region along with carpetbaggers and scalawags, white Republicans from the North and South.

Emancipation changed the stakes of the Civil War; a Union victory would mean a large-scale social revolution in the South thought it was very unclear what form this revolution would take. Over the next several years, Lincoln considered ideas about how to reinstate the devastated South back into the Union. Leading up to the final days of the war in early 1865, Lincoln still had no clear plan; consequently, in a speech delivered on April 11, 1865, he proposed that free blacks and those who had enlisted in the military deserved the right to vote. Lincoln was assassinated three days later, and it would fall to his successor to put plans for Reconstruction in place.

Union victory in the Civil War by 1865 may have given some 4 million slaves their freedom. Consequently, the Reconstruction period (1865-1877) introduced a new set of significant challenges. President Andrew Johnson, between 1865 and 1866, allowed new southern state legislatures to pass the restrictive "black codes" that were designed to control the labor and behavior of former slaves.

The North was outraged over these codes. Support for Presidential Reconstruction was eroded and ultimately led to the triumph of the wing of the Republican Party. During Radical Reconstruction, beginning in 1867, newly enfranchised blacks gained a voice in government for the first time in American history, winning election to southern state legislatures and even to the U.S. Congress. In less than a decade, however, reactionary forces–including the Ku Klux Klan–would reverse the changes wrought by Radical Reconstruction in a violent backlash that restored white supremacy in the South.

Presidential Reconstruction

By May 1865, President Andrew Johnson announced his plans for Reconstruction, which reflected his staunch Unionism and his firm belief in states' rights. Johnson firmly believed that the southern states had never lost their rights to govern themselves, and the federal government should not determine voting requirements or other questions at the state level.

Under Johnson's Presidential Reconstruction, all land that had been confiscated by the Union Army and distributed to the freed slaves by the army or the Freedmen's Bureau (established by Congress in 1865) reverted to its prewar owners. Apart from being required to uphold the abolition of slavery (in compliance with the 13th Amendment to the Constitution), swear loyalty to the Union and pay off war debt, southern state governments were given free rein to rebuild themselves.

As a result of Johnson's leniency, many southern states in 1865 and 1866 successfully enacted a series of laws known as the "black codes," which were designed to restrict freed blacks' activity and ensure their availability as a labor force. These repressive codes enraged many in the North, including numerous members of Congress, which refused to seat Black members of Congress and senators elected from the southern states.

In early 1866, Congress passed the Freedmen's Bureau and Civil Rights Bills and sent them to Johnson for his signature. The first bill extended the life of the bureau, established initially as a temporary organization charged with assisting refugees and freed slaves, while the second defined all persons born in the United States as national citizens who were to enjoy equality before the law.

After Johnson vetoed the bills—causing a permanent rupture in his relationship with Congress that would culminate in his impeachment in 1868—the Civil Rights Act became the first major bill to become law over a presidential veto.

Radical Reconstruction

After northern voters rejected Johnson's policies in the congressional elections in late 1866, Republicans in Congress took firm hold of Reconstruction in the South. The following March, again over Johnson's veto, Congress passed the Reconstruction Act of 1867, which temporarily divided the South into five military districts and outlined how governments based on universal (male) suffrage were to be organized. The law also required southern states to ratify the 14th Amendment, which broadened the definition of citizenship, granting "equal protection" of the Constitution to former slaves, before they could rejoin the Union.

In February 1869, Congress approved the 15th Amendment (adopted in 1870), which guaranteed that a citizen's right to vote would not be denied "on account of race, color, or previous condition of servitude."

By 1870, all of the former Confederate states had been admitted to the Union, and the state constitutions during the years of Radical Reconstruction were the most progressive in the region's history. African-American participation in southern public life after 1867 would be by far the most radical development of Reconstruction, which was primarily a large-scale experiment in interracial democracy unlike that of any other society following the abolition of slavery. Blacks won election to southern state governments and even to the U.S. Congress during this period.

A Radical Change

During the decade known as Radical Reconstruction (1867-77), Congress granted African American men the status and rights of citizenship, including the right to vote, as guaranteed by the 14th and 15th Amendments to the U.S. Constitution. Beginning in 1867, branches of the Union League, which encouraged the political activism of African

Americans, spread throughout the South. During the state constitutional conventions held in 1867-69, blacks and white Americans stood side by side for the first time in political life.

Blacks made up the overwhelming majority of southern Republican voters, forming a coalition with "carpetbaggers" and "scalawags" (derogatory terms referring to the south and north white Republicans, respectively). During that period a total of 265 African-American delegates were elected, more than 100 of who had been born into slavery. South Carolina and Louisiana had the most significant number of elected black delegates because they had the longest history of the political organization; in most other states, African Americans were underrepresented compared to their population. African Americans totaling 16 served in the U.S. Congress during Reconstruction; more than 600 were elected to the state legislatures, and hundreds more held local offices across the South.

The South after the Civil War

By the end of the Civil War, the South's economy, infrastructure, politics, and society mostly in shamble.

Years of warfare had crippled the South's economy, and the abolishment of slavery destroyed what was left. The South's currency was worthless, and its financial system was in ruins. For employers, workers, and merchants, this created many complex problems. With the abolishment of slavery, much of Southern planters' wealth had disappeared. Accustomed to the unpaid labor of slaves, they were faced with the need to pay their workers — but there was little cash available. In this environment, intricate systems of forced labor, which guaranteed cheap labor and ensured white control of that labor, flourished.

For a brief period after the conclusion of fighting in the spring of 1865, Southern whites maintained control of the political system. Desperate to recreate the previous social and economic system and control the movement and freedom of blacks, the white politicians enacted "Black Codes" that denied blacks the rights to testify against whites, to serve on juries or in state militias, or to vote. In response to planters' demands that the freed people be required to work on the plantations, the Black Codes declared that those who failed to sign yearly labor contracts could be arrested and hired out to white landowners. Some states limited the occupations open to blacks and barred them from acquiring land, and others allowed judges to assign black children to work for their former owners without the consent of their parents.

The Birth of Convict Leasing and Peonage

In 1866, Republicans took control of the South's political system and, in what became known as "Reconstruction," attempted to rebuild the South's economy, politics, and culture.

Radical Republicans created the Freedmen's Bureau to offer former slaves food, clothing, and advice on labor contracts. The Thirteenth, Fourteenth and Fifteenth Amendments were passed to attempt to bring equality to blacks. Initially, with federal laws and federal troops offering protection, blacks began to vote and gain political power. The Black Codes were quickly repealed in 1866. However, in 1877, in part because of Northern exhaustion and Southern protests, the federal government withdrew from the South, and black disenfranchisement and unchecked oppression quickly followed.

With Southern whites entirely in power after the federal government pulled out, Southern states began to heavily enforce a series of laws that unfairly penalized poor African Americans for crimes. "Pig laws" made the theft of a farm animal worth a dollar punishable by as much as five years in jail. Vagrancy statutes made it a crime not to have a job or be able to show proof of employment. While these laws did not specifically mention African Americans, they were rarely enforced for whites also resulting in a massive increase in the number of blacks arrested and convicted causing the rise of the labor system known as convict leasing.

CONVICT LEASING

Initially, to save money on prison construction and later to generate revenue, Southern states and counties began leasing "convicts" to commercial enterprises. Within a few years, states realized they could lease out their convicts to local planters or industrialists who would pay minimal rates for the workers and be responsible for their housing and feeding, thereby eliminating costs and increasing revenue. Soon, markets for convict laborers developed, with entrepreneurs buying and selling convict labor leases. From county courthouses and jails, men were leased to local plantations, lumber camps, factories, and railroads. The convict lease system became highly profitable for the states.

To employers and industrialists, these men represented cheap, disposable labor. The costs to lease a laborer were minimal, and the cost of providing housing, food, clothing, and medical treatment could be kept low. Replacement costs were cheap. Unlike in slavery, there was no incentive to treat a laborer well. (Slaves were expensive to purchase, but might create new profit by having children who became more slaves, and could live with a family for generations.)

All Southern blacks view convict leasing with absolute horror. Prisoners were often transferred far from their homes and families. The paperwork and debt record of individual prisoners were often lost; therefore men were unable to prove they had paid their debts; consequently, it was assumed they had not. Working conditions at the convict leasing sites were often terrible: illness, lack of proper food, clothing, or shelter as well as cruel punishments, torture, resulted in unusually high death rates.

Though the profits from convict leasing brought funds to the states' coffers, the public (both Southerners and Northerners) became uncomfortable with the practice of convict leasing. As part of a series of reforms, Alabama created an office of prison inspector to oversee conditions for convict laborers. The inspectors described wretched conditions for convict laborers. New rules for leasing began to require minimum standards for treatment and rules for punishments. These reforms brought only modest improvements.

THE HISTORY OF PEONAGE

Another way that blacks were forced into labor was through a system known as "peonage." Peonage, also called debt slavery or debt servitude, was a system where an employer compelled a worker to pay off a debt with work. Peonage had been in use in New Mexico Territory before the Civil War. Although Congress deemed that peonage was illegal in the Anti-Peonage Law of 1867, the practice began to flourish in the South after Reconstruction.

A loophole in the Thirteenth Amendment that declared involuntary servitude illegal "except as a punishment for crime" was used to trap blacks into peonage.

Defendants were found guilty of real or fabricated crimes and were fined for both the offense and court fees. When the men were unable to pay, a local businessman would step forward to pay the fines. The convict would then sign a contract agreeing to work for the businessman without pay until the debt was paid off.

A second method involved a defendant who, when faced with the likelihood of a conviction and the threat of being sent to a remote work camp, would plead guilty, essentially claiming responsibility before any trial occurred. A local businessman would step forward to act as "surety," vouching for the future good behavior of the defendant, and forfeiting a bond that would pay for the crime. The judge would accept the bond, without ever rendering a verdict on the offense. The defendant would then sign a contract agreeing to work without pay until the surety bond was paid off.

In other cases, workers became indebted to planters (through sharecropping), merchants (through credit) or company stores (through living expenses). Workers were often unable to repay the debt and found themselves in a continuous work-without-pay cycle. Often stuck in remote company towns or on isolated plantations, workers were prevented from attempting escape by chains, cells, guards, dogs, and violence. If they did attempt to flee their workplace or the spurious debt, they risked a very high chance of being picked up, found guilty of abandoning their obligations, fines, Court fees, would eventually be returned to the same employer — or worse, "leased" to a convict mine. There was little interest in prosecuting the employers who abused their forced laborers: the employers were rich, white, and often politically connected. Worse, many of the laborers had "agreed" to their unfair treatment when they signed the contracts were agreeing to work off their debt. Most were unable to read. Sometimes, the contracts stated that the men agreed to be locked up, to be physically punished and that any expenses due to health care, new clothing or re-capturing due to an escape attempt could be added to the total.

Progressivism and the Beginning of the End of Convict Leasing

By the 1890s, blacks in the South were suffering the worst treatment they had endured since the end of the Civil War. After the Supreme Court's 1896 *Plessy v. Ferguson* decision, segregation became even more ensconced through a battery of Southern laws and social customs known as "Jim Crow." Schools, theaters, restaurants, and transportation cars were segregated. Poll taxes, literacy requirements, and grandfather clauses not only prevented blacks from voting but also made them ineligible to serve in jury pools or run for office. "Separate but equal" was not just an unspoken custom, but a formal law.

Meanwhile, a new social and political movement was growing in the North. In response to significant economic, social, and political inequalities, "progressivism" advocated that the government should lead efforts to change society's ills. When President Theodore Roosevelt took office in 1901, progressivism became a powerful national movement. He advocated for fair trade and pro-labor laws, including a decreased workweek, child labor restrictions, and workplace safety rules.

Roosevelt's attitudes towards race fluctuated, though he was generally considered a moderate during his era. As governor of New York, he ended school segregation. As president, Roosevelt invited Booker T. Washington, a black civil rights leader, to dine at the White House. The resulting uproar over the perceived impropriety appeared to restrain Roosevelt, who never repeated the invitation. However, he did continue to advocate for a "square deal" for all citizens, appointing progressive judges and encouraging the prosecution of peonage.

While progressive leaders often focused on the needs of the poor and immigrants, they did *not* organize to promote black suffrage or equal rights for the Advancement of Colored People (NAACP) fought for civil rights.

During this time, dramatic stories of the abuse and wretched conditions of convict laborers began to be publicized through trials and newspaper accounts. The egregiousness of the violence and corruption of the system began to turn public opinion against convict leasing. Public outrage over scandalous tales of abuse led Tennessee to stop leasing convicts to coal mines in 1893 and to stop all rental to all industries by 1896. South Carolina (1897), Louisiana (1901), Mississippi

(1907), Georgia (1908), Arkansas (1913) and Florida (1923) followed suit.

Public concern about eliminating convict leasing did not reflect a desire to create political, economic, or social equality for blacks. During this time, new laws made private peonage even more accessible to establish. Changes to contract labor laws trapped more men into peonage. Alabama peonage was the most persistent. Previously, if a worker skipped out after receiving an advance, an employer had to prove that fraud had always been the worker's intention. Changes in the 1903 law no longer required any evidence of bad intentions by a worker; consequently, white employers could claim a black worker had taken an advance and not repaid it, and Alabama courts would not accept black workers' testimony in court. Georgia passed a similar law in 1903 followed Florida in 1907.

By 1928, Alabama became the final state to eliminate convict leasing by the state.

Chain Gangs

Southern citizens and politicians wanted to abolish convict leasing, the problem of the expense and difficulty of housing convicts remained. Chain gangs were developed as a popular solution to that problem. Chain gangs were groups of convicts forced to labor at tasks such as road construction, ditch digging, or farming while chained together. The improvements they made to public roadways had a significant impact on rural areas, allowing planters to more quickly and efficiently transport their crops to market.

Chain gangs were an efficient labor model because it reduced the cost of guarding prisoners even though it exposed prisoners to painful ulcers and dangerous infections from the oppressive shackles around their ankles.

The Final Chapter of Forced Labor

Throughout the South, new technologies and shifting economic patterns decreased peonage. The dust bowl and the Great Depression moved many sharecroppers off their land. After Franklin Delano Roosevelt was elected, he instituted his "New Deal," a series of economic programs intended to offer relief to the unemployed and recovery of the national economy.

Though blacks were not the intended audience for these programs, they benefitted as many citizens did. Labor laws that encouraged union organization and defined a minimum wage also supported black workers. However, peonage remained — generally hidden in the rural counties of Southern states. In 1940, with the help of the International Labor Defense (ILD), a group of people in New York and Chicago organized the Abolish Peonage Committee and began to pressure the Justice Department to try cases.

In 1941, in response to the outbreak of World War II and amid fears that racial inequalities would be used as anti–United States propaganda, Attorney General Francis Biddle issued Circular No. 3591 to all federal prosecutors, instructing them to investigate and try more peonage cases actively. Finally, the federal government was willing to act aggressively to protect all its citizens from this forced labor.

Summary

By 1619 the first Africans indentured servants arrive in the American colonies. The first slaves were brought into New Amsterdam (later, New York City). By 1690, every colony had slaves. The African population that came over as slaves had begun to reproduce itself by the 1730s through the creation of the African-American population that we call Creole Blacks. These Creole Blacks were the first African Americans, and their process of bridging African and American worlds is what we refer to as creolization. African-Americans Creoles, born after the 1730s, were unlike their ancestors in many respects because they were born in America. African-American-born of the Creole population became dominant after 1820 because African-American culture begins with this Creole population.

True black history has been benchmarked by a series of social engineering events designed to diminish or destroy African American society. We are today, the product of political, social, and legal events at every milestone that African Americans have passed in which something would occur that was either disruptive or destructive.

CHAPTER 2

POST CIVIL WAR (Lynch Time)

The Truth Behind '40 Acres and a Mule'

by Henry Louis Gates, Jr. | Originally posted on The Root

The dream of "40 acres and a mule" to former slaves was the first systematic attempt to provide a form of reparations to newly freed slaves. Black leaders themselves generated the federal government's confiscation of some 400,000 acres - formerly owned by Confederate land owners, and its systematic redistribution to former black slaves. The *400,000 acres* of land comprised "a strip of coastline stretching from Charleston, South Carolina, to the St. John's River in Florida, including Georgia's Sea Islands and the mainland thirty miles in from the coast," as Barton Myers reports — would be redistributed to the newly freed slaves.

General William T. Sherman's Special Field Order No. 15, issued on Jan. 16, 1865 (Sherman had prescribed the 40 acres in that Order, but not the mule. The mule would come later when Sherman reordered that the army could lend the new settlers mules; hence the phrase, "40 acres and a mule." Many accounts leave out the idea for massive land redistribution was the result of a discussion that Sherman and Secretary of War Edwin M. Stanton held four days *before* Sherman issued the Order, with 20 leaders of the black community in Savannah, Ga. where Sherman was headquartered following his famous March to the Sea. The meeting was unprecedented in American history.

Try to imagine how profoundly different the history of race relations in the United States would have been had this policy been implemented and enforced; had the former slaves actually had access to the ownership of land, of property; if they had had a chance to be self-sufficient economically, to build, accrue and pass on *wealth*. After all, one of the principal promises of America was the possibility of average people being able to own *land,* and all that such ownership entailed. As we know all too well, this promise was not to be realized for the overwhelming majority of the nation's former slaves, who numbered about 3.9 million.

A Radical Change

During the decade known as Radical Reconstruction (1867-77), Congress granted African American men the status and rights of citizenship, including the right to vote, as guaranteed by the 14th and 15th Amendments to the U.S. Constitution. Beginning in 1867, branches of the Union League, which encouraged the political activism of African Americans, spread throughout the South. During the state constitutional conventions held in 1867-69, blacks and white Americans stood side by side for the first time in political life.

Reconstruction was a unique era in African-American history when Southern blacks gained the right to hold a political office which resulted in many African-American firsts, like the first black senators and members of the House of Representatives. The federal occupation of the South during the years after the Civil War allowed African-Americans to serve at numerous levels of government, through their political power remained limited.

U.S. Senators

On February 25, 1870, Hiram Revels became the first African-American to serve in Congress as a U.S. Senator. Revels represented the state of Mississippi as a Republican and was born to free black parents in North Carolina. Revels' arrival in the Senate was not without controversy. Some members voted to block his seat, arguing he was not qualified. Despite these initial setbacks, other blacks went on to hold Senate seats during Reconstruction. In 1875, Blanche Kelso Bruce was also elected to the Senate as a Republican from Mississippi. Unlike Revels, Bruce completed a full term in office. During his term, Bruce also supported the seating of Pinckney Pinchback, a black Senator-elect from Louisiana, in Congress, but the Senate voted Pinchback down and refused to seat him. When Bruce left office, he was the last black senator to serve until the 1960s.

U.S. Congressmen

The end of the Civil War also brought numerous blacks to the House of Representatives. Between 1870 and 1887, a total of 17 African-Americans served in Congress. All were Republicans and all represented states in the post-Confederate South. The first black Congressman was Joseph Rainey, a Republican from South Carolina, who was sworn in in 1870. After 1877, the end of Reconstruction reduced blacks' ability to hold political office, and black representatives in Congress declined markedly. No African-Americans, for example, served between 1901 and 1929, and only 22 served in the entire 19th century.

State Legislators

After the Civil War, African Americans had unprecedented access to seats in state legislatures. In total, over 600 blacks served in various Reconstruction Era state legislatures. Besides, blacks briefly comprised the majority in South Carolina's lower house. Black Republicans joined white Northern carpetbaggers to form Republican majorities in all the Southern state legislatures except Virginia's in the years immediately after the Civil War. By the 1870s, however, divisions among Republicans and white resentment led to a substantial decline in black representation in state legislatures.

Executive Offices

While blacks faired reasonably well in legislative positions, state legislatures and the U.S. Congress, they gained less power in administrative positions. In Louisiana, two black men served as Lieutenant Governor in succession: Oliver Dunn followed by P.B.S. Pinchback. When the sitting governor was impeached, Pinchback became the acting governor between December 1872 and January of 1873. Pinchback was the only Black governor of any state during Reconstruction. He was the only black governor in the United States until 1989 when Virginia elected Douglas Wilder. Blacks were denied gubernatorial positions after the Civil War until Wilder.

Background & Risk of Leadership

John Willis Menard appeared tall and lean, dressed in a black suit with tails in an etching from the 1860s. While standing behind an ornate lectern as white members of Congress looked on. He raised his right hand and began: "Mr. Speaker, I appear here more to acknowledge this high privilege than to make an argument before this House." On Nov. 3, 1868, John Willis Menard became the first black man elected to the U.S. House of Representatives. However, Congress refused to seat him.

Those subjects were familiar to Menard, who made history yet was denied what he had earned because of his race. Still, on Feb. 27, 1869, Menard became the first black man to deliver a speech on the floor of the U.S. Congress while Congress was in session. "It was certainly not my intention at first to take any part in this case at all; but as I have been sent here by the votes of nearly 9,000 electors, I would feel recreant to the duty imposed upon me if I did not defend their rights on the floor."

Menard request was heard on the merits of his case and not his race.

Menard had won 64 percent of the vote in a special election in Louisiana to take the seat of James Mann, who had died in office. However, Menard's opponent, a white man named Caleb S. Hunt, protested Menard's right to be seated in Congress, according to House archives.

Both Menard and Hunt were permitted to address Congress. Only Menard took up the offer to make his case before the House. "I wish it to be well understood before I go further that in the disposition of this case I do not expect, nor do I ask, that there shall be any favor shown me on account of my race, or the former condition of that race." Despite his eloquence, Congress refused to admit Menard.

James A. Garfield, the future president who was then a member of Congress, made a motion, saying, "It was too early to admit a Negro to the U.S. Congress, and that the seat was declared vacant, and the salary of $5,000" saved. The seat was left vacant during the remainder of the 40th Congress.

From 1868 to 1898, 22 black men were elected to Congress, including two to the U.S. Senate. After the passage of the 15th Amendment, which granted black men the right to vote and was ratified Feb. 3, 1870, thousands of black men were elected to public offices across the South.

In 1870, Joseph H. Rainey, a Republican from South Carolina, became the first black man to be seated in the House.

Mississippi became the first state to send a black man to the U.S. Senate. Hiram Rhodes Revels served in the 41st Congress from 1870 to 1871, after he was selected by the Mississippi legislature to fill an empty seat, according to a Congressional Research Service report.

"Of particular significance is the fact that all the 17 African-American Members between 1870 and 1887 came from the new Reconstruction governments in the former Confederacy," according to the Congressional Research Service.

However, those numbers dropped precipitously as Jim Crow took root. When Congress convened on Dec. 5, 1887, it was the first time in almost 20 years when no black members were seated.

"All the men who stood up in awkward squads to be sworn in on Monday had white faces," wrote a correspondent for the Philadelphia Record. "The negro is not only out of Congress; he is practically out of politics."

Menard, a poet, and abolitionist, was born April 3, 1838, in the village of Kaskaskia, Ill., to parents of French Creole descent who were free.

Menard, who had attended Iberia College in Ohio, worked as a newspaper editor in Baltimore and Washington and as a clerk in the Department of Interior during the Civil War. President Abraham Lincoln sent Menard to what was then British Honduras in 1863 to study the establishment of a new colony for freed enslaved people, according to the Illinois Historic Preservation Agency.

After the Civil War ended, he went to Jamaica, where he married a Jamaican woman, Elizabeth, and fought for political rights for the British colony's black people. Menard participated in the 1865 Morant Bay Rebellion in Jamaica. He was detained as a political prisoner and deported to the United States. He eventually landed in New Orleans, where he established the newspaper "The Free South."

In 1879, Menard published the book of poetry "Lays in Summer Lands." "Of what avail is life why sigh and fret, When manly hopes are only born to fade? Although declared a man, a vassal yet by social caste a crime by heaven made!" Menard wrote in one of the poems.

Ten years after his book of poetry was published, Menard moved to Washington, where he had been denied his rightful place in Congress. Instead, he worked as a clerk in the U.S. Census office.

Menard died in 1893 is buried in Woodlawn Cemetery in Southeast Washington, where a huge stone also marks the plot for Blanche K. Bruce. Bruce, also born a slave, was the second black man elected to the U.S. Senate — and the first to serve a full term.

Many black leaders during Reconstruction had gained their freedom before the Civil War (by self-purchase or through the will of a deceased owner), had worked as skilled slave artisans or had served in the Union Army. A large number of black political leaders came from the church, having worked as ministers during slavery or in the early years of Reconstruction when the church served as the center of the black community.

Hiram Revels, the first African American elected to the U.S. Senate (he took the Senate seat from Mississippi that had been vacated by Jefferson Davis in 1861) was born free in North Carolina and attended college in Illinois. He worked as a preacher in the Midwest in the 1850s and as a chaplain to a black regiment in the Union Army before going to Mississippi in 1865 to work for the Freedmen's Bureau.

Blanche K. Bruce, elected to the Senate in 1875 from Mississippi, had lived a privileged life as a slave and also received some education. The background of these men was typical of the leaders that emerged during Reconstruction but differed significantly from that of the majority of the African American population.

As the most radical aspect of the so-called Radical Reconstruction period, the political activism of the African American community also inspired the most hostility from Reconstruction's opponents. Because blacks in South Carolina vastly outnumbered whites, the newly-enfranchised voters were able to send so many African American representatives to the state assembly that they outnumbered the whites. Many were able legislators who worked to rewrite the state constitution and pass laws ensuring aid to public education, universal male franchise, and civil rights for all. Though frustrated with policies giving former slaves the right to vote and hold office, Southern whites increasingly turned to intimidation and violence as a means of reaffirming white supremacy. The Ku Klux Klan targeted local Republican leaders and blacks who challenged their white employers, and numerous black officials were murdered by the Klan and other white supremacist organizations during the Reconstruction era.

Some achievements of Reconstruction were the South's first state-funded public school systems, more equitable taxation legislation, laws against racial discrimination in public transport and accommodations and ambitious economic development programs (including aid to railroads and other enterprises).

Reconstruction Comes to an End

However, black political power was short-lived. Northern politicians grew increasingly conciliatory to the white South so that by 1872 virtually all leaders of the Confederacy had been pardoned and were again able to vote and hold office. Utilizing economic pressure and the terrorist activities of violent anti-Black groups, such as the Ku Klux Klan, most African Americans were kept away from the polls. By 1877, when Pres. Rutherford B. Hayes withdrew the last federal troops from the South; Southern whites were again in full control.

African Americans were disfranchised by the provisions of new state constitutions such as those adopted by Mississippi, South Carolina, and Louisiana in 1895. Only a few Southern black elected officials survived. No African American would serve in the U.S. Congress for three decades after the departure of George H. White of North Carolina in 1901.

The rebirth of white supremacy in the South was accompanied by the growth of enforced "racial" separation. Tennessee in 1870, led all the Southern states reenacted laws prohibiting marriage between blacks and whites. They also passed Jim Crow laws segregating blacks and whites in almost all public places. By 1885 most Southern states had officially segregated their public schools. Moreover, in 1896, in upholding a Louisiana law that required the segregation of passengers on railroad cars, the U.S. Supreme Court in the case of Plessy v. Ferguson established the doctrine of "separate but equal."

In the post-Reconstruction years, African Americans received only a small share of the increasing number of industrial jobs in Southern cities. Moreover, relatively few rural African Americans in the South owned their farms, most remaining poor sharecroppers heavily in debt to white landlords. The mostly urban Northern African American population fared little better. The jobs they sought were given to European immigrants. In search of improvement, many African Americans migrated westward.

During and after the Reconstruction period, African Americans in cities organized historical, literary, and musical societies. Literary achievements of African Americans included the Life and Times of Frederick Douglass (1881) which became a classic autobiography. Blacks also began to have a significant impact on American mass culture through the popularity of such groups like the Fisk Jubilee Singers.

The Black Codes Convicts

In 1865 and 1866, state governments in the South enacted laws designed to regulate the lives of the former slaves. These measures, differing from state to state, were revisions of the earlier slave codes that had governed that institution.

Some common elements appeared in many of the Codes: Race was defined by blood; the presence of any amount of black blood made one black. Employment was required of all freedmen; violators faced vagrancy charges. Freedmen could not assemble without the presence of a white person. Freedmen were assumed to be agricultural workers and their duties and hours were tightly regulated. Freedmen were not to be taught to read or write Public facilities were segregated. Violators of these laws were subject to being whipped or branded.

The existence of the black codes was taken as evidence by many Northerners (especially the Radical Republicans) that the South had not been subdued, slavery had merely taken a new form.

The Freedmen's Bureau worked to halt enforcement of many of these laws, and the Republican state governments (imposed by the North) repealed these measures, consequently, when Reconstruction was over, many of the Black Code elements would reappear in Jim Crow legislation.

The Black Codes of 1865

Some of the black codes forced former slaves to sign contracts once the Republican Party took control of Reconstruction, the Black Codes forced former slaves to sign contracts, requiring them to work for meager wages, while some even needed them to work on chain gangs in the fields. Once the Republican Party took control of Reconstruction, they forced the implementation of the Black Codes.

After 1867, an increasing number of southern whites turned to violence in response to the revolutionary changes of Radical Reconstruction. The Ku Klux Klan and other white supremacist organizations targeted local Republican leaders and African Americans who challenged white authority.

Though federal legislation passed during the administration of President Ulysses S. Grant in 1871 took aim at the Klan and others who attempted to interfere with black suffrage and other political rights, white supremacy gradually reasserted its hold on the South after the early 1870s as support for Reconstruction waned. Racism was still a potent force in both South and North, and Republicans became more conservative and less egalitarian as the decade continued.

In 1874–after an economic depression plunged much of the South into poverty–the Democratic Party won control of the House of Representatives for the first time since the Civil War.

When Democrats waged a campaign of violence to take control of Mississippi in 1875, Grant refused to send federal troops, marking the end of federal support for Reconstruction-era state governments in the South. By 1876, only Florida, Louisiana and South Carolina were still in Republican hands.

In the contested presidential election, Republican candidate Rutherford B. Hayes reached a compromise with Democrats in Congress. In exchange for certification of his election, Hayes would acknowledge Democratic control of the entire South. The agreement of 1876 marked the end of Reconstruction as a distinct period, but the struggle to deal with the revolution that was ushered in by slavery's eradication would continue in the South and elsewhere long after that date. Almost a century later, the legacy of Reconstruction would be revived during the civil rights movement of the 1960s, as African Americans demonstrated for the political, economic and social equality that had long been denied.

The U.S. government allowed racist white lynch mobs to murder Black men, women, and children for practically nothing, for years. The lynchings were so absurd that one could argue that Black people's lives were little to no value at all. Most of the lynchings that took place in the South primary reason was the end of the Civil War. Once blacks were given their freedom, many people felt that the freed blacks were getting away with too much freedom and thought they needed to be controlled. Mississippi had the highest number of lynchings from 1882-1968 with 581. Georgia was second with 531, and Texas was third with 493. 79% of lynching happened in the South.

Between 1882 and 1930 in just the ten southern U.S. states of Florida, Tennessee, Arkansas, Kentucky, North Carolina, Mississippi, Georgia, Louisiana, Alabama, and South Carolina, 2,500 black people were lynched. That is an average of nearly one hanging every week.

Below are ten unbelievable reasons Black people were lynched in American history, according to Jana Evans Braziel, Assistant Professor at the University of Cincinnati. Some of them are so startling they are similar to the modern-day killings of Black children by white men, like in the recent cases of Trayvon Martin, wearing his hooded sweatshirt, Jordan Davis, playing loud music at a gas station, or Oscar Grant, merely hanging out at the train station on New Year's Eve.

Vigilante groups were common during the last half of the 19th century and were fed by a strong notion that the existing laws were not functioning correctly resulting in criminals, especially black criminals, being set free at the expense of the public.

A black man was always addressed by his first name or some derogatory term, and he had almost no legal rights. States like Mississippi and Tennessee enacted legislation that was crafted to specifically omit or target African Americans, depending on their purpose.

Ultimately, this would have a demoralizing effect on blacks and made them seem less than human to white society; consequently, this condescension appeared to be officially endorsed by the states. It was easy to mistreat blacks if it could be agreed upon that African Americans were vastly different from whites and not deserving of the same respect. Consequently, this was a result of a disorganized, yet powerful campaign of propaganda carried out by white plantation owners and others who had an economic stake in the retention of cheap black labor. It was to their advantage to keep African Americans in their "place."

In many photos of lynchings at the turn of the century, onlookers and members of the mob can be seen smiling and grinning for the camera. They demonstrate no fear of prosecution or reprisal. They had none, for no white man was ever punished for a lynching until 1915. By then, there had been thousands of lynchings in the South alone with certainly hundreds of thousands of spectators. Some lynchings were even announced in the newspapers beforehand, indicating a strong and undeniable alliance with local law enforcement.

Statistics compiled by the N.A.A.C.P. in 1921 tell the gruesome toll of murders committed in the name of justice. Between the years 1889 through 1918, at least 3,224 people were lynched in America of that number 2,522 were black. The beginning of 1879 saw thousands of African Americans began to migrate out of the South to escape oppression.

Summary

Life under slavery was awful; Emancipation was supposed to eliminate those conditions. Emancipation gifted newly freed slaves with, the rebirth of white supremacy in the South which was accompanied by Black Codes, Chain Gangs, Peonage, Convict Leasing, and finally the Ku Klux Klan. In 1865 and 1866, state governments in the South enacted laws designed to regulate the lives of the former slaves. Between the years 1889 through 1918, at least 3,224 people were lynched in America of that number 2,522 were black. Almost a century later, the legacy of the Emancipation and Reconstruction would be revived during the civil rights movement of the 1960s, as African Americans fought for the political, economic and social equality that had long been denied them.

CHAPTER 3

POST CIVIL WAR ECONOMIC DEVELOPMENT

Great Migration: Life for Migrants in the City

By the end of 1919, 1 million blacks had left the South, often traveling by train, boat, and bus. A determined smaller number had automobiles or even horse-drawn carts. Between 1910 and 1920, the black population of major Northern cities grew significantly including New York(66 percent), Chicago (148 percent), Philadelphia (500 percent)and Detroit (611 percent). Many new arrivals found jobs in factories, slaughterhouses, and foundries, where working conditions were arduous and sometimes dangerous. Female migrants had a harder time finding work, spurring heated competition for domestic labor positions.

Aside from competition for employment, there was also competition for living space in increasingly crowded cities. While segregation was not legalized in the North (as it was in the South), racism and prejudice were nonetheless widespread.

After the U.S. Supreme Court declared racially based housing ordinances unconstitutional in 1917, some residential neighborhoods enacted covenants requiring white property owners to agree not to sell to blacks; these would remain legal until the Court struck them down in 1948.

Rising rents in segregated areas, plus a resurgence of KKK activity after 1915, worsened black and white relations across the country. The summer of 1919 began the most significant period of interracial strife in U.S. history at that time, including a disturbing wave of race riots.

The most serious was the Chicago Race Riot of 1919; it lasted 13 days and left 38 people dead, 537 injured and 1,000 black families without homes.

Impact of the Great Migration

As a result of housing tensions, many blacks ended up creating their cities within big cities, fostering the growth of a new urban, African-American culture. The most prominent example was Harlem in New York City, a formerly all-white neighborhood that by the 1920s housed some 200,000 African Americans.

The Great Migration became an essential theme in the artistic movement known first as the New Negro Movement and later as the Harlem Renaissance, which would have an enormous impact on the culture of the era. The Great Migration also began a new period of increasing political activism among African Americans who after being disenfranchised in the South found a new place for themselves in public life in the cities of the North and West.

Black migration slowed considerably in the 1930s, when the country sank into the Great Depression, but picked up again with the coming of World War II. By 1970, when the Great Migration ended, its demographic impact was unmistakable: Whereas in 1900, nine out of every

10 black Americans lived in the South, and three out of every four lived on farms, by 1970 the South was home to less than half of the country's African-Americans, with only 25 percent living in the region's rural areas.

End of Black Wall Street

In 1921, the Greenwood district neighborhood of Tulsa, Oklahoma, was the site of one of the most devastating massacres in the entire history of the United States. Greenwood was a massacre so ghastly that many chose to forget it, and it was hidden from textbooks and even oral histories for decades. As we struggle today to understand contemporary violence against African Americans, it is especially important to know that history and to try to understand what happened.

Known as "Black Wall Street" to those in the community, Greenwood in the early part of the 20th century was a thriving business district featuring African-American owned businesses, a strong black middle, and upper class, schools, hospitals, and theaters. It was a bustling commercial and social "island" on the Northeast side of Tulsa, Oklahoma.

In just two days in the Spring of 1921, however, it was all destroyed. Put in today's terms, there was $30 million in damage, from fifty-five to 400 killed, 800 injured; family fortunes had evaporated overnight. Many accounts of the demise of Black Wall Street refer to it as a "race riot," but nothing could be further from the truth. It was better described as a *terrorist attack on an affluent black neighborhood*. The armed black men involved were defending their homes, their businesses, and their lives.

Why Tulsa?

Oklahoma, rich in oil deposits, became a state in 1907. It offered a promise of a better life for many formerly enslaved African Americans looking for a chance to start over and get away from the still-repressive Southern states.

In Tulsa, the Frisco railroad tracks divided the "white" part of town from the Greenwood District, called "Little Africa." Laws prevented both whites and blacks from living in neighborhoods that were 75 percent the other race, so segregation "naturally" fell into place.

The oil boom of the 1910s resulted in the construction of beautiful red brick buildings along Greenwood Avenue that was occupied by businesses owned by a thriving black middle class. Theaters, nightclubs, churches, grocery stores thrived in the Greenwood District. The schools were superior to those of the white areas, and many of the houses had indoor plumbing before those in the white areas did.

Because African Americans could not shop in predominately white areas, much money spent in Greenwood went right back into the community. By the time of the attacks on the citizens of Black Wall Street, there were more than 10,000 African Americans living in the area. The community supported two of its newspapers, the Tulsa Star and the Oklahoma Sun—the second covering state and national news and politics as well.

As the community flourished, disgruntlement and hatred did as well. The country was still reeling from the failed Reconstruction and furiously enacting Jim Crow laws. Many African American men in other parts of the United States had been accused of sexual attacks on white women and were subsequently put to death—usually at the hands of a lynch mob. The Ku Klux Klan had approximately 2,000 members in the Tulsa area by the end of 1921. With veterans returning from World War I and jobs becoming more scarce, envy and racial tension grew among some white citizens of Tulsa. Everything came to a terrifying head on May 31 and June 1, 1921.

We are approaching ninety-eighth years since approximately 300 African Americans lost their lives and more than 9,000 were left homeless when the small town was attacked, looted and burned to the ground in 1921. It is impossible, however, to realize what was lost in Greenwood, which was affectionately known as "Black Wall Street."

The 1921 Attack on Greenwood was one of the most significant events in Tulsa's history. Following World War I, Tulsa was recognized nationally for its affluent African American community known as the Greenwood District. This thriving business district and surrounding residential area were referred to as "Black Wall Street." In June 1921, a series of events nearly destroyed the entire Greenwood area.

May 31 – June 1, 1921

On the morning of May 30, 1921, a young black man named Dick Rowland was riding in the elevator in the Drexel Building at Third and Main with a woman named Sarah Page. The details of what followed vary from person to person. Accounts of an incident circulated among the city's white community during the day and became more exaggerated with each telling.

Tulsa police arrested Rowland the following day and began an investigation. An inflammatory report in the May 31 edition of the Tulsa Tribune spurred a confrontation between black and white-armed mobs around the courthouse where the sheriff and his men had barricaded the top floor to protect Rowland. When shots were fired, the outnumbered African Americans began retreating to the Greenwood District.

In the early morning hours of June 1, 1921, Greenwood was looted and burned by white rioters. Governor Robertson declared martial law, and National Guard troops arrived in Tulsa. Guardsmen assisted firefighters in putting out fires, took African Americans out of the hands of vigilantes and imprisoned all black Tulsans not already interned. Over

6,000 people were held at the Convention Hall and the Fairgrounds, some for as long as eight days.

Twenty-four hours after the violence erupted, it ceased. In the wake of the destruction, 35 city blocks lay in charred ruins, over 800 people were treated for injuries, and contemporary reports of deaths began at 36. Historians now believe as many as 300 people may have died.

Race Riot Commission

In 2001, an official Race Riot Commission was organized to review the details of the event. No one will ever know the absolute truth of what happened during the hours of the Race Riot.

However, by examining historical resources, members of the Race Riot Commission determined the number of details to be undeniable. "These are not myths, not rumors, not speculations, not questioned; they are the historical record."

Historical Facts as Determined by the Tulsa Race Riot Commission:

- Black Tulsans had every reason to believe that Dick Rowland would be lynched after his arrest. His charges were later dismissed and highly suspect from the start.
- They had cause to believe that his safety, like the defense of themselves and their community, depended on them alone.
- As hostile groups gathered and their confrontation worsened, municipal and county authorities failed to take actions to calm or contain the situation.
- At the eruption of violence, civil officials selected many men, all of them white and some of the participants in that violence, and made those men their agents as deputies.
- In that capacity, deputies did not stem the violence but added

to it, often through overt acts that were themselves illegal.

- Public officials provided firearms and ammunition to individuals, again all of them white. Units of the Oklahoma National Guard participated in the mass arrests of all or nearly all of Greenwood's residents. They removed them to other parts of the city and detained them in holding centers.
- Entering the Greenwood district, people stole, damaged, or destroyed personal property left behind in homes and businesses.
- People, some of the agents of the government, also deliberately burned or otherwise destroyed homes credibly estimated to have numbered 1,256, along with virtually every other structure — including churches, schools, businesses, even a hospital, and library — in the Greenwood district.
- Despite duties to preserve order and to protect property, no government at any level offered adequate resistance, if any at all, to what amounted to the destruction of the Greenwood neighborhood
- Although the exact total can never be determined, credible evidence makes it probable that many people, likely numbering between 100-300, were killed during the riot.
- Not one of these criminal acts was then or ever has been prosecuted or punished by the government at any level: municipal, county, state, or federal.
- Even after the restoration of order, it was official policy to release a black detainee only upon the application of a white person, and then only if that white person agreed to accept responsibility for that detainee's subsequent behavior.
- As private citizens, many whites in Tulsa and neighboring communities did extend invaluable assistance to the riot's victims, and the relief efforts of the American Red Cross, in particular, provided a model of human behavior at its best.
- Although city and county government bore much of the cost for Red Cross relief, neither contributed substantially to Greenwood's rebuilding, in fact, municipal authorities acted

initially to impede reconstruction.

- Despite being numerically at a disadvantage, black Tulsans fought valiantly to protect their homes, their businesses, and their community. But in the end, the city's African-American population was merely outnumbered by the white invaders.
- In the end, the restoration of Greenwood after its systematic destruction was left to the victims of that destruction.
- While Tulsa officials turned away some offers of outside aid, some individual white Tulsans provided assistance to the city's now virtually homeless black population. But it was the American Red Cross, which remained in Tulsa for months following the riot, that provided the most sustained relief effort. Maurice Willows, the compassionate director of the Red Cross relief, kept a history of the event.

Black Wall Street was modern, majestic, sophisticated and unapologetically Black. Tragically, it was also the site of one of the bloodiest and most horrendous race riots (and acts of terrorism) that the United States has ever experienced. This event marked the end of a prime example of how Black business economic development could/should be, Black Wallstreet never recovered.

Summary

Out-migration from slavery should have been the beginning of a dream based on the initial success of Black Wall Street. Black Wall Street should have been used as the shining example going forward because it represented what Black community building success should look like. Never to be realized again.

CHAPTER 4

SEGREGATION BY SOCIAL ENGINEERING

Cabrini-Green is a Chicago Housing Authority public housing development on Chicago's North Side, bordered by Evergreen Avenue, Sedgwick Street, Division Street, and Larrabee Street. Cabrini-Green, at its peak, was home to Fifteen thousand people who were living in the mid- and high-rise apartment buildings. Over the years, gang violence and city neglect created terrible conditions for the residents, ultimately resulting in the name "Cabrini-Green" becoming synonymous with the problems associated with public housing in the United States.

Though extremely diabolical, the superblock concept was useful in re-segregating Chicago's pre-migration housing. The superblock concept was designed to be a "Honey Trap" for southern migrants that occupied housing throughout most Chicago neighborhoods.

Most of the new public housing that followed, was built in the 1950s and '60s under Mayor Richard J. Daley, came in the form of massive superblocks of high-rise apartments. The superblocks were the answer to integrated housing by concentrating blacks in smaller areas of Chicago. Row after row of monolithic concrete towers was diabolically constructed communities cut off from the neighborhoods around them, forming dense geographic concentrations of poverty. The results would generally prove disastrous. The buildings themselves were often poorly built and difficult to maintain. The massive size of the apartment complexes and a large number of residents made little sense for social order and community impossible to sustain.

By 1968 public housing throughout the city of Chicago was predominantly African American. With high crime and unemployment Cabrini Green, along with other housing projects in the city, came to symbolize the failure of city government in Chicago (and across the nation) to resolve the problems by concentrating and isolating urban African American poor.

Cabrini-Green History

Cabrini–Green was geographically situated in an affluent part of the city. The poverty-stricken projects were constructed at the meeting point of Chicago's two wealthiest neighborhoods, Lincoln Park and the Gold Coast. Less than a mile to the east sat Michigan Avenue with its high-end shopping and expensive housing.

The first part of what would become the vast Cabrini-Green complex was the Frances Cabrini Homes, completed by the Chicago Housing Authority in 1942 was designed to house an influx of Black war-industry workers as well as veterans returning to Chicago during World War II. The Frances Cabrini Homes consisted of 55 two- and three-story buildings in the Near North Side area of Chicago. Those apartment houses were, like the city's other public housing during that era, considered well-built, attractive alternatives to the slums that traditionally housed low-income families.

A turning point for Chicago's public housing occurred in 1950. By that time, those most in need of affordable housing in Chicago were African

Americans, whose numbers were rapidly expanding, primarily because of the northward migration of Southern blacks.

The Robert Taylor Homes, located in the Bronzeville neighborhood of the South Side of Chicago, were at one time the most extensive public housing development in the country. In 1962, the housing developments were named after Robert Taylor, the first Black student to enroll at the Massachusetts Institute of Technology back in 1888.

Composed of 24 16-story high-rises and a total of 4,415 units, the Robert Taylor Homes were once home to Mr. T, athletes Kirby Puckett and Maurice Cheeks, and the recent governor of the state of Massachusetts Deval Patrick.

During its time, the Robert Taylor homes housed some of the poorest residents in the country. A 1999 article reported that 95 percent of the housing development's 20,000 residents were unemployed and listed public assistance as their only income source. With such poverty, the Robert Taylor Homes recorded some of the highest rates of violent crime and gang activity in Chicago.

Cabrini-Green, a public housing development in Chicago, Illinois was once a model of successful public housing, but poor planning, and managerial neglect, coupled with gang violence, drugs, and chronic unemployment, turned it into a national symbol of urban blight and failed housing policy.

In 1970, two police officers were killed by a sniper in one of the buildings. In the decades that followed, despite a variety of efforts to increase security, the police department had very little motivation to secure Cabrini-Green. Gangs, drugs, and sensational crimes controlled individual buildings, while residents felt pressure to ally with those gangs to protect themselves from escalating violence.

During the worst years of Cabrini–Green's problems, vandalism increased substantially. Gang members and miscreants covered interior walls with graffiti to identify territory. Rat and cockroach infestations were commonplace, rotting garbage stacked up in clogged trash chutes, occasionally pilling up to the 15th floor, and basic utilities (water, electricity, etc.) often malfunctioned and were left unrepaired.

The building's exterior had boarded-up windows, burned-out areas of the façade, and concrete paved areas instead of green space, all efforts used to reduce maintenance cost, all of which created an atmosphere of decay and government neglect. In an aim of preventing residents from emptying garbage cans into the yard, the balconies were fenced. Fencing also prevented people from falling or being thrown to their deaths. The results were the appearance of a large prison tier, or animal cages, which enraged the residents.

Finally, public transportation in the region ended. The high rise structures became unmanageable for the police, so they abandoned them to gang violence and drugs that created terrible conditions for the 15000 residents that lived in Cabrini-Green. Most of the superblock residents who had moved to south Chicago- brought the Cabrini Green culture with them. The high crime/murder rate that is a daily occurrence in South Chicago is used as the example of Black culture, Black values even though some refuse to acknowledge that it is the result of a brilliant social engineering plan by Mayor Richard M. Daily and staff.

First, you isolate people. Next, you neglect their basic needs. Finally, you refuse to provide social structure (police), and ultimately they will become self-destructive animals, the Cabrini Project was a success.

Fast forward to 2016; Southside Chicago had become Cabrini Green with a homicide count in 2016 of 762 people.

Throughout the following years, the Cabrini Green project became a social engineering model for housing segregation.

Summary

Cabrini Greene, the end of the migration dream, represented the devastating effects of racial, social engineering. After the U.S. Supreme Court declared 1888 racially based housing ordinances unconstitutional in 1917, some residential neighborhoods enacted covenants requiring white property owners to agree not to sell to blacks; these would remain legal until the Court struck them down in 1948. Segregation released the creative spirits of those who would oppress and dominate the weak and defenseless. Thus Cabrini Greene.

CHAPTER 5

IMPACT OF BROWN V BOARD OF EDUCATION

The1954 Supreme Court unanimous decision for the Brown v. Board of Education case ruled segregation in public schools was unconstitutional. The result was a white flight from inner cities which reduced tax support for the public school system, thus causing an underfunded black educational system. The effects are continuing to be felt today through low performing black students.

BACKGROUND OF HISTORICALLY BLACK COLLEGES AND UNIVERSITIES

Before the Civil War, there was no structured education system for black students. Public policy and specific local laws prohibited the education of blacks in various parts of the nation. The Institute for Colored Youth, the first higher education institution for blacks, was founded in Cheyney, Pennsylvania, in 1837. It was followed by two other black institutions--Lincoln University, in Pennsylvania (1854), and Wilberforce University, in Ohio (1856) both have survived to today.

Although these institutions were called universities" or "institutes" from their founding, a significant part of their mission in the early years was to provide elementary and secondary schooling for students who had no previous education. It was not until the early 1900s that HBCUs began to offer courses and programs at the postsecondary level.

Following the Civil War, public support for higher education for black students was reflected in the enactment of the Second Morrill Act in 1890. The Act required states with racially segregated public higher education systems to provide a land-grant institution for black students whenever a land-grant institution was established and restricted for white students. After the passage of the Act, public land-grant institutions specifically for blacks were found in each of the southern and border states. This act resulted in some new public black institutions being founded, and some formerly private black schools came under federal control; eventually, 16 black institutions were designated as land-grant colleges. These institutions offered courses in agricultural, mechanical, and industrial subjects, but few provided college-level courses and degrees.

The U.S. Supreme Court's 1896 decision in Plessy v. Ferguson established a "separate but equal" doctrine in public education, invalidating racially dual public elementary and secondary school systems, Plessy also encouraged black institutions to focus on teacher training to provide a pool of instructors for segregated schools. Subsequently, the expansion of black secondary schools reduced the need for black colleges to offer college preparatory instruction.

U.S. Schools were legally desegregated in 1954 by the Supreme Court decision of Brown vs. Board of Education, which overturned Plessy vs. Ferguson law which supported the principle that educational facilities are inherently unequal.

Groups of African American students like "Little Rock Nine" began to enter previously "all-white" schools, and thus began the long process of desegregation in American public schools. Though the U.S. school system still struggles with issues relating to fair education of African American children, the nation has certainly come a long way since the founding of Winter Park's first "colored" schoolhouse in 1890.

By 1953, more than 32,000 students were enrolled in such well known private black institutions as Fisk University, Hampton Institute, Howard University, Meharry Medical College, Morehouse College, Spelman College, and Tuskegee Institute, as well as a host of smaller black colleges located in southern and border states. In the same year, over 43,000 students were enrolled in public black colleges. HBCUs enrolled 3,200 students in graduate programs. These private and public institutions mutually served the critical mission of providing education for teachers, ministers, lawyers, and doctors for the black population in a racially segregated society.

The addition of graduate programs, mostly at public HBCUs, reflected three Supreme Court decisions in which the "separate but equal" principle of Plessy was applied to graduate and professional education. The choices stipulated: (1) a state must offer to school for blacks as soon as it provided one for whites (Samuel v. Board of Regents of the University of Oklahoma, 1948); (2) black students must receive the same treatment as white students (MacLaurin v. Oklahoma State Regents, 1950); and (3) a state must provide facilities of comparable quality for black and white students (Sweatt v. Painter, 1950). Black students increasingly were admitted to traditionally white graduate and professional schools if their program of study was unavailable at HBCUs. In effect, desegregation in higher education began at the post-baccalaureate level.

In 1954, the U.S. Supreme Court decision in Brown v. Board of Education rejected the "separate but equal" doctrine and held that racially segregated public schools deprive black children of equal protection guaranteed by the Fourteenth Amendment of the United States Constitution. The Plessy decision, which had governed public education policy for more than a half-century, was overturned.

Despite the landmark Supreme Court decision in Brown, most HBCUs remained segregated with poorer facilities and budgets compared with traditionally white institutions. Lack of adequate libraries and scientific and research equipment and capabilities placed a severe handicap on many. Many of the public HBCUs closed or merged with traditionally white institutions. However, most black college students continued to attend HBCUs years after the decision was rendered.

CIVIL RIGHTS ACT OF 1964

Soon after the Brown decision, Congress passed Title VI of the Civil Rights Act of 1964 to provide a mechanism for ensuring equal opportunity in federally assisted programs and activities. In enacting Title VI, Congress also reflected its concern with the slow progress in desegregating educational institutions following the Supreme Court's Brown decision. Title VI protects individuals from discrimination based on race, color, or national origin in programs or activities receiving federal financial assistance. Passage of the law led to the establishment of the Office for Civil Rights (OCR) in the former Department of Health, Education, and Welfare (HEW). OCR placed its primary compliance emphasis in the 1960s and early 1970s on eliminating unconstitutional elementary and secondary school segregation in the southern and border states.

EARLY COMPLIANCE ACTIVITY IN POSTSECONDARY

Nineteen states were operating racially segregated higher education systems at the time Title VI was enacted. In 1969-70, after intensive investigative work, OCR notified a number of the states that they violated Title VI for having failed to dismantle their previously operated segregated systems of higher education. OCR sought, without success, statewide higher education desegregation plans. In 1970, private plaintiffs filed suit against HEW for failing to initiate enforcement action against the systems under investigation by OCR. Their lawsuit is known as the Adams case.

In 1977, as part of the Adams case, a court ordered the federal government to establish new, uniform criteria for statewide desegregation. In response, OCR published rules specifying the ingredients of acceptable plans to desegregate State systems of public higher education (Criteria). The Criteria recognized the unique role of HBCUs in meeting the educational needs of black students. Accordingly, the Criteria called for the enhancement of HBCUs through improvements in physical plants and equipment, number and quality of faculties, and libraries and other financial support. The Criteria also called for expanding nonminority enrollment at HBCUs by offering on their campuses academic programs that are in high demand or unavailable at the state systems' other schools. Efforts also were to be made to provide HBCUs with resources that would ultimately ensure they were at least comparable to those at traditionally white institutions having similar missions.

Under the plans accepted by OCR, HBCUs have aimed for desegregated student enrollments and better programs and facilities while retaining or enhancing their historical stature. OCR has monitored the plans to make sure they have been implemented.

ACCOMPLISHMENTS OF HBCUs

Under the plans, substantial progress has been made by many states in the desegregation of their state systems of higher education. At the same time, HBCUs continue to be a vital resource in the nation's educational system. Among their accomplishments are the following:

- HBCUs played a historical role in enhancing equal educational opportunity for all students.
- More than 80 percent of all black Americans who received degrees in medicine and dentistry were trained at the two traditionally black institutions of medicine and dentistry--Howard University and Meharry Medical College. (Today, these institutions still account for 19.7 percent of degrees awarded in medicine and dentistry to black students.)
- HBCUs have provided undergraduate training for three-fourths of all black persons holding a doctorate; three-fourths of all black officers in the armed forces; and four-fifths of all black federal judges.
- HBCUs are leading institutions in awarding baccalaureate degrees to black students in the life sciences, physical sciences mathematics, and engineering.
- HBCUs continue to rank high in terms of the proportion of graduates who pursue and complete graduate and professional training.

Fifty percent of black faculty in traditionally white research universities received their bachelor's degrees at an HBCU.

HBCU graduates include Mary McLeod Bethune, educator and founder of Bethune Cookman College W.E.B. DuBois, sociologist, educator, and co-founder of the NMCP. Charles Drew, physician and medical researcher; Patricia Harris, former Secretary, U.S. Departments of Health, Education, and Louis Sullivan, Secretary, U.S. Department of Health and Human Services Welfare and Housing and Urban Development; Martin Luther King, Jr., recipient of the Nobel Peace Prize, Thurgood Marshall, Supreme Court Justice; Christa McAuliffe, first educator in space graduated from Bowie State U.; Kenneth B. Clark, psychologist;

Leontyne Price, world-renowned opera soprano; and many black political leaders.

Today, there are 107 HBCUs with more than 228,000 students enrolled. Fifty-six institutions are under private control, and 51 are public colleges and universities. The public institutions account for more than two-thirds of the students in historically black institutions. Most (87) of the institutions are four-year colleges or universities, and 20 are two-year institutions. In the past, more than 80 percent of all black college graduates have been trained at these HBCUs. Today, HBCUs enroll 20 percent of black undergraduates. However, HBCUs award 40 percent of baccalaureate degrees earned by black college students.

WHITE HOUSE INITIATIVE ON HISTORICALLY BLACK COLLEGES AND UNIVERSITIES

On April 28, 1989, President George Bush issued Executive Order 12677 to strengthen the capacity of HBCUs to provide quality education and to increase their participation in federally sponsored programs. It mandates the taking of positive measures, by federal agencies, to increase the participation of HBCUs, their faculty and students, in federally sponsored programs. It also encourages the private sector to assist HBCUs. The Executive Order was administered by the Department's Office of Postsecondary Education - White House Initiative on Historically Black Colleges and Universities. This office also coordinates the activities of 27 federal departments and agencies in implementing Executive Order 12677. These agencies were selected for participation in the program because they account for 98 percent of federal funds directed to our colleges and universities.

HIGHER EDUCATION ACT

Title III of the Higher Education Act of 1965, as amended, authorizes funds for enhancing HBCUs. The statute allows the "Strengthening Historically Black Colleges and Universities Program" and the "Strengthening Historically Black Graduate Institutions Program." Title III is administered by the Department's Office of Postsecondary Education - Division of Institutional Development.

CONSIDERING AN HBCU

Selecting a college in which to enroll is a very personal choice. However, HBCUs offer a valuable option for minority and nonminority students alike. Some of the factors that make HBCUs attractive include:

- Cost
  Many HBCUs have lower tuition and fees compared to traditionally white institutions. A number also offer a broad spectrum of financial assistance to qualified students and have extensive experience in identifying sources of financial support for deserving students. Financial aid may come in the form of scholarships, loans, and grants to cover the cost of tuition, fees, room and board, books, supplies, personal expenses, and transportation.

- Cultural and Racial Diversity
  HBCUs often serve students from a wide range of cultural and socioeconomic backgrounds. Students interested in the humanities, or such areas as sociology, psychology, economics, government, urban planning, etc., may find their exposure to a broader range of individuals and their cultures particularly valuable.

  Nonresident aliens constitute a large portion of the student enrollment at many HBCUs. Many international students and professors at HBCUs participate in student or faculty exchange programs. In general, HBCUs endeavor to be sensitive to the needs of international students and provide those students with an opportunity to associate with different nationalities and to learn about cultural diversities.

Multicultural exposures are expected to become increasingly valuable as the demographics of the American workforce change and America competes more aggressively in the world economy.

Today many HBCUs have a racially diverse students enrollment at the undergraduate and graduate levels. Also, the majority of HBCUs continue to have a racially diverse faculty and administration. HBCUs are presently more racially desegregated, relative to their enrollment and staff, than traditionally white institutions.

- Remediation and Retention
  HBCUs may offer a more supportive educational setting for students encountering some difficulty in realizing their full academic potential. HBCUs generally provide a broad range of effective remedial programs for students.

  Many HBCUs have established developmental centers, reading laboratories, and expanded tutorial and counseling services to accommodate the unique needs of educationally disadvantaged students. The result was a strong commitment by many HBCUs to serve all students with a high rate of graduation.

- Faculty Support
  Traditionally, the faculties at many HBCUs place as much, or more, emphasis on teaching and student service-oriented activities as on research, thus permitting more time for personal and high-quality student-teacher interactions. Many teachers

at HBCUs have experience in working with minority students and students from diverse socioeconomic backgrounds. Research findings indicate that these factors are essential for the academic success of many minority students.

- New Programs
  As a result of the desegregation plans approved by OCR under Title VI, many state systems of higher education have placed new high demand programs and curricula-such as engineering, pharmacy, and computer science-at HBCUs.

  Students considering options in postsecondary education faced one of the most difficult and important choices of their lives. Their decisions should lead to informed selections reflecting the broadest possible range of educational opportunities. HBCU provide those opportunities.

Summary

The Washington, D.C. public school system before integration, was an example of a productive teaching/learning for black children. That system used the considerable advantage that segregation created, the highest educated black professionals had few opportunities for employment. Thus they turned to education. The result was that the researcher (W.W. Cooksey) on the team that developed the "Polio Vaccine" taught science at Douglas Jr. high school. Those kids were blessed with college-level teaching.

Many other factors that made D.C. the public school system productive was the use of skills/interest focused based teaching. This system consisted of three learning tracts, college prep., general learning, and trades and crafts.

Those students that focused on college were taught at the academic challenge that would prepare them for college. Kids that were not interested in higher education were ready for the local job market. Then there was those, who were only interested in working with their hands in the trades and craft job market. These kids learn to be carpenters, electricians, plumbers, and auto mechanics. Thus, every kid that graduated from high school was prepared for the job market.

When school de-segregation started, the Black community focused only on college-level preparation, which ultimately lost most black students. Only (10% to 20%) of black kids desired to pursue a college education while forgetting who wished to develop useful skills at the end of high school. Those who drove the education agenda had two goals; integrate immediately, because "white schools were better," teach only academic skills because all black kids should be intellectuals, not service providers. The result was a large portion of black students failed to meet minimum academic standards- they had little interest.

CHAPTER 6

DESTRUCTIVE EFFECTS OF CIVIL RIGHTS ACT OF 1964

History of the Civil Rights Act 1875

The drafting of the bill was performed early in 1870 by Senator Charles Sumner, a dominant Radical Republican in the Senate, with the assistance of John Mercer Langston, a prominent African American who established the law department at Howard University. The bill was proposed by Senator Sumner and co-sponsored by Representative Benjamin F. Butler, both Republicans from Massachusetts, in the 41st Congress of the United States in 1870. Congress removed the coverage of public schools that Sumner had included. The act was passed by the 43rd Congress in February 1875 as a memorial to honor Sumner, who had just died. It was signed into law by U.S. President Ulysses S. Grant on March 1, 1875.

President Grant had wanted an entirely different law to help him suppress election-related violence against blacks and Republicans in the South. Congress did not grant his request but instead wrote a bill for equal rights to public accommodations were passed as a memorial to Grant's bitterest enemy, the late Senator Charles Sumner Grant never commented on the 1875 law and did nothing to enforce it says historian John Hope Franklin. Grant's Justice Department ignored it and did not send copies to US attorneys, says Franklin, while many federal judges called it unconstitutional before the Supreme Court shut it down. Franklin concludes regarding Grant and Hayes administrations, "The Civil Rights Act was never effectively enforced," since white public opinion was opposed, while the black community was in support. Historian Rayford Logan looking at newspaper editorials finds the press was overwhelmingly opposed. Thus, the first attempt at a comprehensive Civil Rights Bill was an abject failure. The journey to the final Civil Rights Amendment was a long, multi-faceted, and costly one.

Let's start with a few contrasting numbers.

In 1940, 60 percent of employed black women worked as domestic servants; today the number is down to 2.2 percent, while 60 percent hold white- collar jobs.

In 1958, 44 percent of whites said they would move if a black family became their next-door neighbor; today the figure is 1 percent.

In 1964, the year the great Civil Rights Act was passed, only 18 percent of whites claimed to have a friend who was black; today 86 percent say they do, while 87 percent of blacks assert they have white friends.

Progress is the largely suppressed story of race and race relations over the past half-century. And thus it's news that more than 40 percent of African Americans now consider themselves members of the middle class. Forty-two percent own their own homes, a figure that rises to 75 percent if we look just at black married couples. Black two-parent families earn only 13 percent less than those who are white. Almost a third of the black population lives in suburbia.

Because these are facts the media seldom report, the black underclass continues to define black America in the view of much of the public. Many assume blacks live in ghettos, often in high-rise public housing projects. Crime and the welfare check are seen as their primary source of income. The stereotype crosses racial lines. Blacks are even more prone than whites to exaggerate the extent to which African Americans are trapped in inner-city poverty. In a 1991 Gallup poll, about one-fifth of all whites, but almost half of black respondents, said that at least three out of four African Americans were impoverished urban residents. And yet, in reality, blacks who consider themselves to be middle class outnumber those with incomes below the poverty line by a wide margin.

A Fifty-Year March out of Poverty

Authors Abigail Thernstrom, Stephan Thernstrom
Senior Fellow, Manhattan Institute

More than seventy-five years ago most blacks were indeed trapped in poverty, although they did not reside in inner cities. When Gunnar Myrdal published An American Dilemma in 1944, most blacks lived in the South and on the land as laborers and sharecroppers. (Only one in eight owned the land on which he worked.) A trivial 5 percent of black men nationally were engaged in nonmanual, white-collar work of any kind; the vast majority held ill-paid, insecure, manual jobs— jobs that few whites would take. As previously noted, six out of ten African-American women were household servants who, driven by economic desperation, often worked 12-hour days for pathetically low wages. Segregation in the South and discrimination in the North did create a sheltered market for some black businesses (funeral homes, beauty parlors, and the like) that served a black community barred from patronizing "white" establishments. But the number was minuscule.

In the 1940s, profound demographic and economic changes took place, accompanied by a marked shift in white racial attitudes, started blacks down the road to much greater equality. New Deal legislation, set minimum wages and hours and eliminated the incentive of southern employers to hire low-wage black workers, put a damper on further industrial development in the region. In addition to the trend toward mechanized agriculture and diminished demand for American cotton on the world market, and higher international competition combined to displace blacks from the land.

As a consequence, with the shortage of workers in northern manufacturing plants following the outbreak of World War II, southern blacks in search of jobs boarded trains and buses in a Great Migration that lasted through the mid-1960s. They found what they were looking for: wages so strikingly high that in 1953 the average income for a black family in the North was almost twice that of those who remained in the South. And through much of the 1950s wages rose steadily and unemployment was low.

Thus by 1960 only one out of seven black men still labored on the land, and almost a quarter was in white-collar or skilled manual occupations. Another 24 percent had semiskilled factory jobs that meant membership in the stable working class, while the proportion of black women working as servants had been cut in half. Even those who did not move up into higher-ranking jobs were doing much better.

A decade later, the gains were even more striking. From 1940 to 1970, black men cut the income gap by about a third, and by 1970 they were earning (on average) roughly 60 percent of what white men took in. The advancement of black women was even more impressive. Black life expectancy went up dramatically, as did black homeownership rates. Black college enrollment also rose—by 1970 to about 10 percent of the total, three times the prewar figure.

In subsequent years these trends continued, although at a more leisurely pace. For instance, today more than 30 percent of black men and nearly 60 percent of black women hold white-collar jobs. Whereas in 1970 only 2.2 percent of American physicians were black, the figure is now 4.5 percent. But while the fraction of black families with middle-class incomes rose almost 40 percentage points between 1940 and 1970, it has inched up only another 10 points since then.

Affirmative Action Doesn't Work

Rapid change in the status of blacks for several decades followed by a definite slowdown that begins when affirmative action policies get their start: that story certainly seems to suggest that racial preferences have enjoyed an inflated reputation. "There's one simple reason to support affirmative action," an op-ed writer in the New York Times argued in 1995. "It works." That is the voice of conventional wisdom.

In fact, not only did significant advances pre-date the affirmative action era, but the benefits of race-conscious politics are not clear. Significant differences (a slower overall rate of economic growth, most notably) separate the pre-1970 and post-1970 periods, making comparison difficult.

We know only this: some gains are probably attributable to race-conscious educational and employment policies. Preferences "worked" for these beneficiaries, in that they were given seats in the classroom that they would not have won in the absence of racial double standards.

Black colleges and university professors more than doubled between 1970 and 1990; the number of physicians tripled; the number of engineers almost quadrupled, and the number of attorneys increased more than sixfold. Those numbers undoubtedly do reflect the fact that the nation's professional schools changed their admissions criteria for black applicants, accepting and often providing financial aid to

African-American students whose academic records were much weaker than those of many white and Asian-American applicants whom these schools were turning down.

On the other hand, these professionals make up a small fraction of the total black middle class. And their numbers would have grown without preferences, the historical record strongly suggests. Also, the most significant economic gains for African Americans since the early 1960s were in the years 1965 to 1975 and occurred mainly in the South, as economists John J. Donahue III and James Heckman have found. Donahue and Heckman discovered "virtually no improvement" in the wages of black men relative to those of white men outside of the South over the entire period from 1963 to 1987, and southern gains, they concluded, were mainly due to the critical anti-discrimination provisions in the 1964 Civil Rights Act.

Concerning federal, state, and municipal set-asides, as well, the jury was still out. In 1994 the state of Maryland decided that at least 10 percent of the contracts it awarded would go to minority- and female-owned firms. It more than met its goal. The program, therefore "worked" if the goal was merely the narrow one of dispensing cash to a particular, designated group. But how well do these sheltered businesses survive long-term without extraordinary protection from free-market competition? And with almost 30 percent of black families still living in poverty, what was their trickle-down effect? On neither score was the picture reassuring. Programs were often fraudulent, with white contractors offering minority firms 15 percent of the profit with no obligation to do any of the work. Alternatively, set-asides enriched those with the right connections. In Richmond, Virginia, for instance, the main effect of the ordinance was a marriage of political convenience—a working alliance between the economically privileged of both races. The white business elite signed on to a piece-of-the-pie for blacks to polish its image as socially conscious and secure support for the downtown revitalization it wanted. Black politicians used the bargain to suggest their importance to low-income constituents for whom the set-asides did little. Neither cared whether the policy provided real economic benefits—which it didn't.

Has the Engine of Progress Stalled?

In the decades since affirmative action policies were first instituted, the poverty rate has remained unchanged. Despite black gains by numerous other measures, close to 30 percent of black families still live below the poverty line. "There are those who say, my fellow Americans, that even good affirmative action programs are no longer needed," President Clinton said in July 1995. But "let us consider," he went on, that "the unemployment rate for African Americans remains about twice that of whites." Racial preferences are the president's answer to persistent inequality, although a quarter-century of affirmative action has done nothing whatever to close the unemployment gap.

Persistent inequality is serious, and if discrimination were the primary problem, then race-conscious remedies might be appropriate. White racism was central to the story in 1964; today the picture is much more complicated. Blacks and whites now graduate at the same rate from high school today and are almost equally likely to attend college; on average, they are not similarly educated. Looking at years of schooling in assessing the racial gap in family income tells us little about the cognitive skills whites and blacks bring to the job market because cognitive abilities affect earnings.

The National Assessment of Educational Progress (NAEP) is the nation's report card on what American students attending elementary and secondary schools know. Those tests show that African-American students, on average, are alarmingly far behind whites in math, science, reading, and writing. For instance, black students at the end of their high school career are almost four years behind white students in reading; the gap is comparable in other subjects. A study of 26- to 33-year-old men who held full-time jobs in 1991 thus found that when education was measured by years of school completed, blacks earned 19 percent less than comparably educated whites. But when word knowledge, paragraph comprehension, arithmetical reasoning, and mathematical knowledge became the yardstick, the results were reversed. Black men earned 9 percent more than white men with the same education— that is, the same performance on basic tests.

Other research suggests much the same point. For instance, the work of economists Richard J. Murnane and Frank Levy has demonstrated the increasing importance of cognitive skills in our changing economy. Employers in firms like Honda now require employees who can read and do math problems at the ninth-grade level at a minimum. And yet the 1992 NAEP math tests, for example, revealed that only 22 percent of African-American high school seniors but 58 percent of their white classmates were numerate enough for such firms to consider hiring them. And in reading, 47 percent of whites in 1992 but just 18 percent of African Americans could handle the printed word well enough to be employable in a modern automobile plant. Murnane and Levy found a clear impact on income. Not years spent in school, but strong skills made for high long-term earnings.

The Widening Skills Gap

Why is there such a glaring racial gap in levels of educational attainment? It is not easy to say. The gap, in itself, is terrible news, but even more alarming is the fact that it has been widening in recent years. In 1971, the average African-American 17-year-old could read no better than the typical white child who was six years younger. The racial gap in math in 1973 was 4.3 years; in science, it was 4.7 years in 1970. By the late 1980s, however, the picture was notably brighter. Black students in their final year of high school were only 2.5 years behind whites in both reading and math and 2.1 years behind on tests of writing skills.

Had the trends of those years continued, by today black pupils would be performing about as well as their white classmates. Instead, black progress came to a halt, and serious backsliding began. Between 1988 and 1994, the racial gap in reading grew from 2.5 to 3.9 years; between 1990 and 1994, the racial disparity in math increased from 2.5 to 3.4 years. In both science and writing, the racial divide has widened by a full year.

There is no obvious explanation for this alarming turnaround because the early gains had very much to do with the growth of the black middle class, but the black middle class did not suddenly begin to shrink in the late 1980s. The poverty rate was not dropping significantly when educational progress was occurring, nor was it on the increase when the racial gap began once again to widen. The considerable rise in out-of-wedlock births and the steep and steady decline in the proportion of black children growing up with two parents do not explain the fluctuating educational performance of African-American children. It is well established that children raised in single-parent families do less well in school than others, even when all other variables, including income, are controlled. But the disintegration of the black nuclear family—presciently noted by Daniel Patrick Moynihan as early as 1965—was occurring rapidly in the period in which black scores were rising so it cannot be invoked as the main explanation as to why scores began to fall many years later.

Some would argue that the initial educational gains were the result of increased racial integration and the growth of such federal compensatory education programs as Head Start. But neither desegregation nor compensatory education seems to have increased the cognitive skills of the black children exposed to them. In any case, the racial mix in the typical school has not changed in recent years, and the number of students in compensatory programs and the dollars spent on them has kept going up.

What about changes in the curriculum and patterns of course selection by students? The educational reform movement that began in the late 1970s did succeed in pushing students into a "New Basics" core curriculum that included more English, science, math, and social studies courses. There was a good reason to believe that taking tougher courses contributed to the temporary rise in black test scores. This observation nicely fits the facts for the period before the late 1980s but not the very different picture after that. The number of black students going through "New Basics" courses did not decline after 1988, pulling down their NAEP scores.

They were left with three tentative suggestions. First, the increased violence and disorder of inner-city lives that came with the introduction of crack cocaine and the drug-related gang wars in the mid-1980s most likely had something to do with the reversal of black educational progress. Chaos in the streets and within schools affects learning inside and outside the classroom.

Also, an educational culture that has increasingly turned teachers into guides who help children explore whatever interests them may have affected black academic performance as well. As educational critic E. D. Hirsch, Jr., has pointed out, the "deep aversion to and contempt for factual knowledge that pervade the thinking of American educators" means that students fail to build the "intellectual capital" that is the foundation of all further learning. That will be particularly true of those students who come to school most academically disadvantaged—those whose homes are not, in effect, an additional school. The deficiencies of American education hit hardest those most in need of education.

And yet in the name of racial sensitivity, advocates for minority students too often dismiss both common academic standards and standardized tests as culturally biased and judgmental. Such advocates have plenty of company. Christopher Edley, Jr., professor of law at Harvard and

President Clinton's point man on affirmative action, for instance, has allied himself with testing critics, labeling preferences the tool colleges are forced to use "to correct the problems we"'ve inflicted on ourselves with our testing standards." Such tests can be abolished—or standards lowered—but once the disparity in cognitive skills becomes less evident, it is harder to correct.

Closing that skills gap was the first task if black advancement was to continue at its once-fast pace. Raise the level of black educational performance, and the gap in college graduation rates, in attendance at selective HBCU schools, and in earnings is likely to close as well. Moreover, with educational parity, the whole issue of racial preferences disappears.

The Road to True Equality

Black progress over the past half-century has been impressive, conventional wisdom to the contrary. Thurgood Marshall said in 1992, "I wish I could say that racism and prejudice were only distant memories, but as I look around I see that even educated whites and African American… have lost hope inequality." A year earlier The Economist magazine had reported the problem of race as one of "shattered dreams." All hope has not been "lost," and "shattered" was much too strong a word, but certainly in the 1960s, the civil rights community failed to anticipate just how tough the voyage would be. (Thurgood Marshall had envisioned an end to all school segregation within five years of the Supreme Court s decision in Brown v. Board of Education.) Many blacks, particularly, are now discouraged. A 1997 Gallup poll found a sharp decline in optimism since 1980; only 33 percent of blacks (versus 58 percent of whites) thought both the quality of life for blacks and race relations had gotten better.

Thus, progress—by many measures seemingly so clear—is viewed as an illusion, the sort of fantasy to which intellectuals are particularly prone. But the ahistorical sense of nothing gained is in itself bad news. Pessimism is a self-fulfilling prophecy. If all our efforts as a nation to resolve the "American dilemma" have been in vain—if we've been spinning our wheels in the rut of ubiquitous and permanent racism, as Derrick Bell, Andrew Hacker, and others argue—then racial equality is a hopeless task, an unattainable ideal. If both blacks and whites understand and celebrate the gains of the past, however, we will move forward with the optimism, insight, and energy that further progress surely demands.

Summary

The Civil Rights Act of 1964 ended segregation in public places and banned employment discrimination by race, color, religion, sex or national origin, was considered one of the crowning legislative achievements of the civil rights movement. The truth was that the Civil Rights Act bought black America heroin, crack cocaine and the beginning of the end of intact black families. African Americans had become a society of drug addicts that continue to this day, ultimately preventing them from participating in developing wealth.

Progress is the largely suppressed story of race and race relations over the past half-century. And thus it's news that more than 40 percent of African Americans now consider themselves members of the middle class. Forty-two percent own their own homes, a figure that rises to 75 percent if we look just at black married couples. Black two-parent families earn only 13 percent less than those who are white. Almost a third of the black population lives in suburbia.

Because these are facts the media seldom report, the black underclass continues to define black America in the view of much of the public. Many assume blacks live in ghettos, often in high-rise public housing projects. Crime and the welfare check are seen as their primary source of income. The stereotype crosses racial lines. Blacks are even more prone than whites to exaggerate the extent to which African Americans are trapped in inner-city poverty. In a 1991 Gallup poll, about one-fifth of all whites, but almost half of black respondents, said that at least three out of four African Americans were impoverished urban residents. And yet, in reality, blacks who consider themselves to be middle class outnumber those with incomes below the poverty line by a wide margin.

CHAPTER 7

WELFARE THE BEGINNING OF THE END OF INTACT BLACK FAMILIES

Until early in the year of 1965, the news media was conveying only whites as living in poverty when suddenly that perception had changed to blacks. Some of the influences in this shift could have been the civil rights movement and urban riots from the mid-60s. Welfare had then shifted from being a White issue to a Black issue and during this time frame; the war on poverty had already begun. Subsequently, news media portrayed stereotypes of Blacks as lazy, undeserving and welfare queens. The social engineering design of Welfare was to remove blacks from workforce competition by giving them a free check with the following requirements; only women qualified, no man (father) could live in the house receiving a free check."Thus began the end of the intact family."

How racism has shaped the welfare policy in America since 1935

Alma CartenAugust 22, 2016
Alma Carten, New York University

Historically, UNICEF reports found that the U.S. ranked 34th on the list of 35 developed countries surveyed on the well-being of children. The Pew Institute found that children under the age of 18, are the most impoverished age population of Americans, while African-American children are almost four times as likely as white children to be in poverty.

These findings were alarming, not least because they came on the 20th anniversary of President Clinton's promise to "end welfare as we know it" with his signing on August 23, 1996, the Personal Responsibility and Work Opportunity Reconciliation Act (P.L. 104-193).

At that time the data would show the number of families receiving cash assistance fell from 12.3 million in 1996 to current levels of 4.1 million as reported by The New York Times. However, it was also true that child poverty rates for black children remained stubbornly high in the U.S.

Research indicated that this did not happen by chance. An examination of social welfare policy developed in the U.S. over 50 years from 1935 to the 1996 reforms revealed that U.S. welfare policies have, from their very inception, been discriminatory.

Blemished by a history of discrimination

The 1935 Social Security Act (SSA), introduced by the Franklin Roosevelt administration, first committed the U.S. to the safety net philosophy.

From the beginning, the policy had two tiers that intended to protect families from loss of income.

On one level were the contributory social insurance programs that provided income support to the surviving dependents of workers in the event of their death or incapacitation and Social Security for retired older Americans.

The second tier was made up of means-tested public assistance programs that included what was initially called the "Aid to Dependent Children" (ADC) program and was subsequently renamed the Aid to Families with Dependent Children in the 1962 Public Welfare Amendments to the SSA under the Kennedy administration.

The optimistic vision of the architects of the ADC program was that it would die "a natural death" with the rising quality of life in the country as a whole, resulting in more families becoming eligible for the work-related social insurance programs. However, this scenario was problematic for black Americans because of pervasive racial discrimination in employment in the decades of the 1930s and 1940s. During these decades, blacks typically worked in menial jobs that were not tied to the formal workforce, they were paid in cash and "off the books," making them ineligible for social insurance programs that called for contributions through payroll taxes from both employers and employees.

Blacks did not fare much better under ADC during those years because ADC was an extension of the state-operated mothers' pension programs, where white widows were the primary beneficiaries. The criteria for eligibility and need were state-determined, so blacks continued to be barred from full participation because the country operated under the "separate but equal" doctrine adopted by the Supreme Court in 1896.

Jim Crow Laws and the separate but equal doctrine resulted in the creation of a two-track service delivery system in both law and custom, one for whites and one for blacks that were anything but fair.

In the 1950s and '60s, black families were further disadvantaged with Jim Crow Laws that happened when states stepped up efforts to reduce ADC enrollment and costs. Residency requirements were proposed to bar blacks migrating from the South to qualify for the program. New York City's "man in the house rule" required welfare workers to make unannounced visits to determine if fathers were living in the home – if evidence of a male presence was found, cases were closed and welfare checks discontinued.

Always an unpopular program because of strong American work ethic, and preference for a "hand up" versus a "hand-out," the means-tested, cash assistance programs for poor families – and especially ADC re-named AFDC – have never been popular among Americans. As FDR himself said in his 1935 State of the Union address to Congress, "the government must and shall quit this business of relief."

As the quality of life did indeed improve for whites, the number of white widows and their children on the AFDC rolls declined. At the same time, the easing of racial discrimination widened eligibility to more blacks, increasing the number of never-married women of color and their children who were born out of wedlock.

One point, however, to note here is that there has always been a public misconception about race and welfare. It is true that over the years blacks became disproportionately represented. However, given that whites constitute a majority of the population, numerically they have always been the largest users of the AFDC program.

The retreat from the safety net philosophy can be dated to the presidencies of Richard Nixon and Ronald Reagan.

On the one hand, politicians wanted to reduce the cost of welfare. Under Reagan policies of New Federalism, social welfare expenditures were capped, and responsibility for programs for low-income families was given back to states.

On the other hand, the demographic shift in the welfare rolls exacerbated the politics around welfare and racialized the debate.

Ronald Reagan's "Welfare Queen" narrative only reinforced existing white stereotypes about blacks: "There's a woman in Chicago. She has 80 names, 30 addresses, 12 Social Security cards and is collecting veterans' benefits on four nonexistent deceased husbands. She has got Medicaid, is getting food stamps and welfare under each of her names. Her tax-free cash income alone is over $150,000."

Reagan's assertions that the homeless were living on the streets by choice played to conventional wisdom about the causes of poverty, blamed poor people for their misfortune and helped disparage government programs to help the poor.

By the late 1990s efforts of reforms targeting the AFDC program shifted to more nuanced forms of racism with claims that the program encouraged out-of-wedlock births, irresponsible fatherhood, and intergenerational dependency. The political context for the 1996 reforms, fueled racist undertones that played into public angst about rising taxes and the national debt. The1996 specific reforms were attributed to the high payout of welfare checks to people who were not carrying their weight. It emotionally charged the poverty debate that resulted in a reform bill that many saw as excessively punitive in its harsh treatment of low-income families.

Although credited to the Clinton administration, the blueprint for the 1996 welfare reform bill was crafted by a caucus of conservative Republicans led by Newt Gingrich as part of the Contract with America during the 1994 congressional election campaign.

Twice President Clinton vetoed the welfare reform bill sent to him by the GOP-dominated Congress. The third time he signed it, creating much controversy, including the resignation of his adviser on welfare reform, the leading scholar on poverty David Ellwood.

The new bill replaced the AFDC program with Temporary Assistance to Needy Families (TANF). Stricter work requirements required single mothers to find work within two years of receiving benefits. A five-year lifetime limit was imposed for receiving benefits. To reinforce traditional family values, a core principle of the Republican Party, teenage mothers were to be prohibited benefits, and fathers who were delinquent in child support payments were threatened with imprisonment. States were banned from using federally funded TANF for certain groups of immigrants and restrictions were placed on their eligibility to Medicaid, food stamps and Supplementary Social Security Income (SSI).

The Impact

Despite many gloomy predictions, favorable outcomes were reported on the 10th anniversary of the bill's signing. Welfare rolls had declined. Mothers had moved from welfare to work, and children had benefited psychologically from having an employed parent.

However, the volume of research generated at the 10-year benchmark has not been matched by that produced in years leading up to the 20th anniversary.

More research, in particular, is needed to understand what is happening with families who have left welfare rolls because of passing the five-year lifetime limit for receiving benefits but have not sustained a foothold in an ever-increasing specialized workforce.

Disentangling intertwined effects of racism and poverty

U.S. welfare policy is, arguably, as much a reflection of its economic policies as it is of the nation's troublesome history of racism.

In the words of President Obama, racism is a part of America's DNA and history. Similarly, the notion that anyone who is willing to work hard can be productive is just as much a part of that DNA. Both have played an equal role in constraining adequate policy development for needy families and have been especially harmful to poor black families.

Racism has left an indelible mark on American institutions. In particular, it influences how we understand the causes of poverty and how we develop solutions for ending it. Indeed, with the continual unraveling of the safety net, the 20th anniversary of welfare reforms can be an impetus for taking a closer look at how racism has shaped welfare policy in the U.S. and to what extent it accounts for the persistently high poverty rates for black children.

Summary

New York City's "man in the house rule" required welfare workers to make unannounced visits to determine if fathers were living in the home – if evidence of a male presence was found, cases were closed and welfare checks discontinued. Thus the beginning of the end of intact black families.

It is true that over the years blacks became disproportionately represented. However, given that whites constitute a majority of the population, numerically they have always been the largest users of the AFDC program.

Ronald Reagan's "Welfare Queen" narrative only reinforced existing white stereotypes about blacks: "There's a woman in Chicago. She has 80 names, 30 addresses, 12 Social Security cards and is collecting veterans' benefits on four nonexistent deceased husbands. She has got Medicaid, is getting food stamps and welfare under each of her names. Her tax-free cash income alone is over $150,000."\

The Clinton bill replaced the AFDC program with Temporary Assistance to Needy Families (TANF). Stricter work requirements required single mothers to find work within two years of receiving benefits. A five-year lifetime limit was imposed for receiving benefits. To reinforce traditional family values, a core principle of the Republican Party, teenage mothers were to be prohibited benefits, and fathers who were delinquent in child support payments were threatened with imprisonment.

Despite many gloomy predictions, favorable outcomes were reported on the 10th anniversary of the bill's signing. Welfare rolls had declined. Mothers had moved from welfare to work, and children had benefited psychologically from having an employed parent.

President Obama once stated that "Racism has left an indelible mark on American institutions. In particular, it influences how we understand the causes of poverty and how we develop solutions for ending it."

CHAPTER 8

WAR ON DRUGS (Mass Incarceration of Black of Males)

The "War on Drugs" was mass incarceration, was the national policy of locking up millions of black offenders. Long before 1994, the national frenzy for punishment endorsed the"three strikes mandatory minimums," and "truth in sentencing with the latter being a euphemism for "no parole." Today there is a significant push to deal with the mass incarceration problem because it no longer affects the black community. Now, the Opiate addicted white population is the most impacted.

John Ehrlichman, the chief domestic adviser to President Richard Nixon and Watergate co-conspirator, admitted in an interview with Dan Baum that was recounted in a 2016 Harper's Magazine interview:

The Nixon campaign in 1968 and the Nixon White House had two enemies: the anti-war left and black people. "You understand what I'm saying"? We knew we couldn't make it illegal to be either against the war or blacks, but by getting the public to associate the hippies with marijuana and blacks with heroin, and then criminalizing both heavily, we could disrupt those communities. We could arrest their leaders, raid their homes, break up their meetings, and vilify them night after night on the evening news. Did we know we were lying about the drugs? Of course, we did.

Poverty, police, and prisons—for too many black, brown and indigenous communities, was where you find one, you see the others.

If you have a white woman who has developed a heroin problem and she's selling a little bit of heroin to maintain her habit, somebody might say, 'Oh, this poor woman; we need to get her in a program because she's not a dealer.' You can take a black woman in the same situation, it'll conjure up all the myths of crack moms, and black women are terrible mothers, as she gets the book thrown at her."

Black and brown people are four times as likely to be arrested for marijuana possession than their white counterparts. Black and brown communities are blatantly targeted using broken-windows policing and surveillance. Despite the New York City Police Department's fraudulent claim; their Police department is one of the biggest perpetrators of these racist tactics.

Now that opioid addiction is at epidemic levels and considered a crisis for white America, politicians have called for a "gentler" war on drugs that protects white drug users (and sellers) while still criminalizing black users and sellers.

When former New Jersey Gov. Chris Christie discussed his compassionate approach to the ongoing opioid epidemic, he would frequently bring up a close friend from law school. He describes this friend as perfect — incredibly smart, with a successful law practice, with a beautiful and brilliant wife and kids, and both good looking *and* athletic. "So we loved him, but we hated him," Christie joked at a 2015 town hall. "Because the guy had everything, right?" "He's a drug addict. And he couldn't get help. And now he's dead." He added, "When I sat there as the governor of New Jersey at his funeral, and looked across the pew at his three daughters sobbing 'cause their dad was gone, there but for the grace of God go I. It can happen to anyone; therefore, we need to start treating people in this country, not jailing them. We need to give them the tools they need to recover because every life is precious."

The drug overdose epidemic has not hit people of all racial groups; equally, white Americans are suffering far more overdose deaths than their black and Latino peers. This epidemic is a dramatic racial shift from before the 2000s when past drug crises tended to hit black, urban communities much harder.

One reason for the disparity may, ironically, be racism against nonwhite Americans. Studies show that doctors are more reluctant to prescribe painkillers to minorities because doctors mistakenly believe that minority patients feel less pain or are more likely to misuse and sell drugs. Perversely, this shielded minority patients from the tsunami of opioid painkiller prescriptions that got white Americans hooked on opioids and led to a wave of deadly overdoses.

The opioid epidemic was primarily responsible for the record 52,000 drug overdose deaths reported in 2015. Since the crisis has disproportionately affected white Americans, white lawmakers are more likely to come into contact with people afflicted by the opioid epidemic than, the disproportionately black drug users who suffered during the crack cocaine epidemic of the 1970s, 80s, and 90s. Consequently, a lawmaker is perhaps more likely to have the kind of interaction that Christie, Trump, Bush, and Fiorina described — a supportive and more compassionate drug policy — in the current crisis than the ones of old. Between 1999 and 2015, more than 560,000 people in the US died of drug overdoses, a death toll more extensive than the entire population of Atlanta.

Police chiefs in the cities most affected by heroin are responding differently than during the Black epidemic, by not by invoking military metaphors, weapons, and tactics but by ensuring that police officers save lives and get people into rehab. As one former narcotics officer described his change of heart on addiction, "These are people, and they have a purpose in life and we cannot as law enforcement look at them any other way." In his inability to name the change that allowed this epiphany, his words also capture our cringe-worthy self-denial. Suddenly, police officers understand crime as a sign of underlying addiction requiring coordinated assistance, rather than a scourge to be eradicated by locking up Black folk.

It is hard to describe the bittersweet sting that many African-Americans feel witnessing this national embrace of addicts. It is heartening to see the eclipse of the generations-long failed war on drugs. Black Americans are weary and embittered by the absence of such sympathetic thinking when those in our own families were similarly inflicted. When the face of addiction had dark skin, this nation's police did not see sons and daughters, sister and brothers. They saw "brothas," young thugs to be locked up, rather than people with a purpose in life, and an illness.

Who Uses Heroin? Not Whom You Might Think

The profile of the typical heroin user has changed over the past 50 years. In the1960s and 1970s, heroin users were primarily inner-city young men from minority groups. Today, the population most likely to get hooked on heroin are white men and women in their late 20s living outside of large urban areas.

The historical profile was that" heroin use was confined to a small area in the inner cities among minority populations," in a study authored by Theodore J. Cicero, a professor of psychiatry at Washington University in St. Louis. Today it is moved beyond that," to the suburbs and rural areas."

As heroin use has moved from predominantly lower-income urban locations to middle-class suburbs and rural communities, the public health issue of heroin addiction has become more widespread. (Heroin use is still a problem among lower-income city men.) [10 Easy Paths to Self-Destruction] The findings were published online yesterday (May 28) in the journal JAMA Psychiatry.

Emerging trends

In a study, researchers analyzed survey data from nearly 2,800 men and women throughout the United States who had sought treatment for their heroin addiction. Cicero and his colleagues wanted to determine who was using heroin, why they were using it and how patterns of opioid abuse (heroin or prescription opioids) had changed over the past five decades.

One new trend emerged along racial lines: White individuals made up approximately 90 percent of the study participants who began using heroin in the last decade.

Gender-based differences were also seen: Men represented slightly more than 80 percent of heroin users who began their opioid abuse in the 1960s, according to the study. However, by 2010, nearly equal numbers of male and female heroin users were seeking treatment.

The analysis also found that heroin users are getting a little older. The age of first use of heroin or any opioid has gradually increased, from age 16 in the 1960s to 23 in 2010.

Many "new" heroin users were once prescription-drug abusers. In middle-class areas, Cicero explained, people were using prescription opioids — such as OxyContin, Vicodin, and Percocet — to get high with increasing frequency since the 1990s. However, in 2010, when drug manufacturers introduced an abuse-deterrent formulation of OxyContint had made it harder for addicts to extract the active drug or to inject or inhale, prescription painkillers became more expensive and difficult to obtain.

Consequently, heroin use became the cheaper and more accessible alternative to prescription opioids, Cicero said. "Heroin use is following prescription drug abuse," he told Live Science.

When heroin use hit the Suburbs

By Stephen Lerner and Nelini Stamp May 16, 2014

Stephen Lerner is a fellow at Georgetown University's Kalmanovitz Initiative and the architect of the Justice for Janitors campaign. Nelini Stamp is the youth engagement director for Working Families.

In 2014, NBC News ran a series of stories about the United States' "growing heroin epidemic." Two things stood out in the report: One is their sympathetic tone; the other is that almost everyone depicted is white. Drug users and their families were not vilified; there is no panicked call for police enforcement. Instead, and appropriately, there is a call for treatment and rehabilitation. Parents of drug addicts express love for their children, and everyone agrees they need support to get clean.

In one NBC report, a drug court judge kindly cajoles and encourages people into getting treatment to avoid jail time. Another shows a teacher who was shooting up in the school bathroom now off drugs and happily married. Parents talk passionately about the need to have access to Naloxone, a drug that can counteract heroin overdoses. Every user was treated as a human being who made a mistake and who, with the proper support, can go on to live a productive life.

The heroin epidemic has exploded in white America. The Post has reported on its arrival in affluent Fairfax County, where "young people are jeopardizing their futures with a drug that for decades had been seen as the choice of only the most desperate and hardened city junkies." Peter Shumlin (D), the governor of Vermont — one of the whitest states — devoted his entire State of the State address this year to the effect of opiate addiction on Vermonters and what government could do to help them.

New attention to heroin use in white, affluent areas is changing the perceptions and politics of drug addiction. No longer are the addicts "desperate and hardened." Heroin use is no longer the result of bad parenting; or the rise of single-parent families or something sick or deviant in white culture. It is not an incurable plague that is impossible to treat except with jail time. Drug addicts no longer are predatory monsters. In short, the root problem is not the degeneration of a group of Americans. The use of heroin has spread — the National Survey on Drug Use and Health reported that America had 373,000 users in 2007 and 669,000 in 2012 — and the increase was primarily attributed to heroin is much cheaper than prescription opiates, which are harder to get legally and increasingly expensive on the black market. Economics are driving white suburban addiction, not the dysfunction that is often attributed to communities of color when those young people abuse drugs.

You cannot help but wonder how the story of a black teacher in an inner-city school shooting drugs in the school bathroom would be characterized. Alternatively, how the heroin addiction of a single black mother with two sons would always be depicted on the nightly news.

We do not have to wonder: We know exactly how drug use had been depicted and responded to when it was perceived chiefly as a problem in communities of color. The 1973 Rockefeller drug laws in New York mandated a minimum sentence of 15 years to life in jail for selling two ounces or possessing four ounces of heroin. The federal government followed suit in the 1980s with mandatory minimum sentencing as part of its "war on drugs."

The media responded to the 1980s crack epidemic with countless stories of incurable "crack babies" who would inevitably grow up to be criminals. The "culture of poverty" welfare queens and poor people were themselves the cause of drug abuse, and the only solution to protect society (read: white society) was swift, harsh and unrelenting punishment and long jail sentences.

We can only hope that the sympathy was shown to white, often affluent, young heroin users will add momentum to the calls to roll back the destructive incarceration policies that hurt the country as a whole and have disproportionately impacted communities of color. The district attorney for Brooklyn plans to stop prosecuting people arrested for possession of small amounts of marijuana, and marijuana is being decriminalized and legalized across the country.

The Obama administration announced a pathway to clemency for some nonviolent drug offenders. These are baby steps in the right direction to start the reverse of one of the most significant causes of mass incarceration of people of color.

Racially different drug enforcement and sentencing is just one part of a larger story about growing economic and racial inequality in the U.S. legal system. To live to the "creed of equal justice under the law," we either have to reform our drug laws or lock up all those nice Fairfax County kids and throw away the key.

Summary

The Nixon campaign in 1968 and the Nixon White House had two enemies: the anti-war left and black people. John Ehrlichman stated in a radio interview: "We knew we couldn't make it illegal to be either against the war or blacks, but by getting the public to associate the hippies with marijuana and blacks with heroin, and then criminalizing both heavily, we could disrupt those communities."

The media's portrayal of the African American community during the 1980s crack epidemic with countless stories of incurable "crack babies" who would inevitably grow up to be criminals. The "culture of poverty" welfare queens and poor people were themselves the cause of drug abuse, and the only solution to protect (white society) was swift, harsh and unrelenting punishment and long jail sentences through the "War on Drugs."

Between 1999 and 2015, more than 560,000 people in the US died of opioid drug overdoses, and a death toll is larger than the entire population of Atlanta. The annual white death rate since then is approx. 50,000 annually.

Now that opioid addiction is at epidemic levels and considered a crisis for white America, politicians have called for a "gentler" war on drugs that protects white drug users (and sellers), through the Criminal Justice Reform Act.

White drug users and their families are not vilified; there is no panicked call for police enforcement. Instead, and appropriately, there is a call for treatment and rehabilitation. Parents of drug addicts express love for their children, and everyone agrees they need support to get clean.

In one NBC report, a drug court judge kindly cajoles and encourages people into getting treatment to avoid jail time. Another shows a teacher who was shooting up in the school bathroom now off drugs and happily married. Parents talk passionately about the need to have access to Naloxone, a drug that can counteract heroin overdoses. It was felt that if every user was treated as a human being who made a mistake and who, with the proper support, can go on to live a productive life.

There was one positive outcome of the Criminal Justice Reform initiative, the " Mass Incarcerated Black" individuals were given reduced sentences, restored citizenship rights, and the right to vote. It should never be foolishly believed that the Criminal Justice Reform Act had anything to do with Black people. It was the realization that the opioid epidemic would cause mass incarceration of white drug offenders as did Crack did to the Black community.

Summary

John Ehrlichman, the chief domestic adviser to President Richard Nixon and Watergate co-conspirator, admitted in an interview with Dan Baum that was recounted in a 2016 Harper's Magazine interview:

> The Nixon campaign in 1968 and the Nixon White House had two enemies: the anti-war left and black people. "You understand what I'm saying"? We knew we couldn't make it illegal to be either against the war or blacks, but by getting the public to associate the hippies with marijuana and blacks with heroin, and then criminalizing both heavily, we could disrupt those communities. We could arrest their leaders, raid their homes, break up their meetings, and vilify them night after night on the evening news. Did we know we were lying about the drugs? Of course, we did.

Poverty, police, and prisons—for too many black, brown and indigenous communities, was where if you find one, you see the others.

CHAPTER 9

TRUE HISTORY OF BLACK ECONOMIC DEVELOPMENT A (1 Trillion GPD Economy)

History of the Black Economy

January 27, 1865, John W. Alvord, a Congregational minister and abolitionist met in New York with other leaders to explore the idea of establishing a savings bank that would benefit African American soldiers during the Civil War. African Americans were receiving back pay and bounties for serving in the war lacked a place to deposit their monies and were victimized by swindlers.

After several attempts by Alvord to open a savings bank, a bill to incorporate the Freedman's Savings and Trust Company was bought before Congress. On March 3, 1865, President Abraham Lincoln signed into law "An Act to Incorporate the Freedman's Savings and Trust Company."

In 1874 changes to the loan and investment policy resulted from the panic of 1873 due to overexpansion, mismanagement, abuse, and fraud the Freedman's Bank finally put it on the road to collapse. Frederick

Douglass invested $10,000 of his own money but soon realized the bank's imminent failure he recommended to Congress the bank to be closed.

One reason for the bank's failures was the increasing speculative investment along with adding a new bank in Washington, D.C. A second example was an ill-advised loan by Freedmen's bank to Seneca Sandstone Company. Seneca Quarry held an unsecured loan during the panic of 1873. Ultimately, Seneca Quarry defaulted on the loan.

June 20, 1874, Congress authorized the trustees to appoint a three-member board to take charge of the bank and report its finding. Only a short time later the bank was closed.

The bank closing was a devastating blow to the African American community. During this time there were 37 branches in 17 states. The most demeaning economic nightmare was when the depositors believed the federal government protected their deposits. Not only did many lose their monies but lost their hope for the future, henceforth losing their trust in banks. Many of the depositors received only three-fifths of the value of their accounts; others received nothing.

Freedman's Bank & Trust concept begins with the African American soldiers, farmers, African American churches, private businesses, and the beneficial societies maintained accounts. These organizations encouraged their members to open accounts. When the bank failed, these organizations that were so vital to the community had to discontinued services, adding to the economic downfall.

The Trillion Dollar African American Consumer Market

The generally accepted view of Black America is one of rampant poverty. Nothing could be farther from the truth. In 2013 the agreed value of the African American GDP (gross domestic product) was 1.3 Trillion dollars. GDP(gross domestic product), is the market value of all final goods and services purchased by a nation in a given year.

- Over the past hundred years, African Americans have gained visibility and importance as a consumer market. During this same period, African Americans would lose much of their traditional business infrastructure. From an economic standpoint, this is especially disturbing because it is *most* advantageous to be a *producer*, as well as a *consumer*.

- Collectively the African American net income (spending power) now exceeds 1 trillion dollars annually. Because of this economic reality, a wide variety of contemporary companies continually create marketing campaigns to reach this critical segment of the U.S. consumer market effectively. In the not-too-distant past, black consumers were mostly ignored in the American marketplace.

- World War I brought the first Great Migration of rural southern blacks to northern and mid-western cities was to take war-related jobs, was followed by an even more massive migration of southern blacks to the north, and western cities during World War II created a viable African American consumer market. By the end of World War II, blacks were strategically located in America's major urban markets with money to spend. Consequently, white companies began to think in terms of a distinctly African American consumer market worth pursuing.

- *By 2013, the African American consumer market exceeded the trillion dollar mark for the first time. When you put this figure in perspective, the market was larger than the market for the entire nation of Spain. In an article by business historian Robert Weems briefly describes the rise of African American purchasing power since the end of slavery and its impact for both black Americans and the entire economy.*

Sub-Prime Nightmare

Families typically spend more as house values increase and they can borrow against their equity. Then, as prices fell and credit was tightened, they would spend less. For a time, up until the sub-prime meltdown, equity withdrawals acted as an engine of growth to the economy. The opposite was true in 2007; the sharp drop in housing prices had become a drag on the African American economy. Real home equity fell 6.5 percent to $9.6 trillion in 2007. The 2008 State of the Nations Housing study reports that there was a switch from housing appreciation to depreciation, additionally the 2007 slowdown in home equity withdrawals, reduced about one-half of a percentage point from real consumer spending and more than one-third of a percentage point from total economic growth. The worse yet to come.

SUB-PRIME RACIAL TARGETING

The changes in the mortgage market, of which the current sub-prime meltdown is the most visible part of a larger pattern, were not racially neutral. Sub-prime loans were targeted at the African American community. With the recognition that average American families were accumulating trillions of dollars in housing wealth, "financial innovation" soon followed. New financial instruments, which relaxed and sometimes ignored rules and regulations, became the market's answer to broadening homeownership.

The housing industry-promoted picture of sub-prime as an instrument of home-ownership opportunity for moderate-income buyers was highly misleading. First, homeownership rates reached their historic highs before the zenith of sub-prime lending; and, second, increased access to credit brought homeownership opportunities within reach of groups that had historically been denied access to credit. The real issue ultimately became the actual terms of the loan.

Today, many critics now describe the sub-prime crisis as a consequence of bad loans to unqualified borrowers while the issue needed to be re-framed to focus on the onerous terms of these loans. The Community Advantage Program, a partnership of Self-Help, Fannie Mae, and the Ford Foundation analysis show that home loans to riskier populations, like lower-income, minority, and single-headed households, do not default at significantly higher rates than conventional loans as long as they are not the handiwork of predators.

The difference is that loans through the Community Advantage Program had terms that were closer to conventional mortgages as opposed to the risky terms that have characterized sub-prime mortgages. Sub-Prime loans had high hidden costs, exploding adjustable rates, and prepayment penalties to preclude refinancing. When lower-income families had similar terms of credit as conventional buyers and were linked with a community-based social and organizational infrastructure that helps them become ready for home-ownership, they pay same interest rates and default at similar rates.

PREDATORY LENDING AND WEALTH STRIPPING

Redlining is a term used for an illegal practice where people living in a particular area or neighborhood are not given the same access to credit as people in other areas or communities by race, color, or for some other prohibited reason. Though the practice had been illegal for decades, it still goes on today.

Minority communities received a disproportionate share of sub-prime mortgages. As a result of Redlining, minorities are suffering a dispro-portionate burden of the harm and losses. According to a De¯mos report, *Beyond the Mortgage Meltdown* (June 2008), in addition to being the target of mortgage companies specializing in sub-prime lending, minorities were steered away from safer, conventional loans by bro-kers who received incentives for jacking up the interest rate. Worst of all, African Americans who qualified for conventional mortgages were steered to riskier, and more profitable, sub-prime loans.

Households of color were more than three times as likely as white households to end up with riskier loans with features like exploding adjustable rates, deceptive teaser rates, and balloon payments. Good credit scores often made no difference, as profit incentives trumped sound policy. The line from redlining to sub-prime was direct as was the blame; even many upper-income African Americans were steered into sub-prime mortgages.

The Center for Responsible Lending (and other groups) projects that 2.2 million borrowers who bought homes between 1998 and 2006 will lose their houses and up to $164 billion of wealth in the process. African American and Latino homeowners are twice as likely to suffer sub-prime-related home foreclosures as white homeowners are. Foreclosures are projected to affect one in 10 African American borrowers. In contrast, only about one in 25 white mortgage holders will be affected. African Americans and Latinos are not only more likely to have been caught in the sub-prime loan trap; they are also far more dependent, as a rule, on their homes as financial resources.

The De͞mos report finds that home equity, at its current total value of $20 trillion, represents the most significant source of wealth for most Americans, and, as we have noted, it is even more important for African Americans. The comparatively little bit of wealth accumulation in the African American community was mainly concentrated in housing wealth.

One recent estimate places the total loss of wealth among African American households at between $72 billion and $93 billion for sub-prime loans taken out during the past twelve years.

Forty years after the Fair Housing Act of 1968, housing markets are still segregated by class and race, realtors polite reference to location,

location, location. Homes appreciate most in value when they were situated in predominantly white communities. They appreciate least in value when located in the low-income minority or integrated communities, except when those communities undergo gentrification (and often become mostly white).

This perverse market logic was also reflected in the sub-prime crisis. Sub-prime loans and foreclosures are not randomly distributed but spatially concentrated in low-to-moderate income communities, especially minority communities. Thus, the wealth-stripping phenomenon, of which sub-prime lending schemes are the latest financial innovation to tap new sources of wealth, is even more devastating in African American and minority communities. In turn, foreclosures and the terms of credit in African American neighborhoods bring down home values in the community as a whole. The community impact adds a community level to the personal tragedies and downstream consequences.

This devastating impact was not confined to just those who have suffered foreclosures; there is a spillover effect in addition to the direct hit of 1.27 million foreclosures. An additional 40.6 million neighboring homes will experience devaluation because of sub-prime foreclosures that take place in their community.

The Center for Responsible Lending estimates that the total decline in house values and the tax base from nearby foreclosures will be $202 billion. The direct hit on housing wealth for homeowners living near foreclosed properties will cause property values to decrease by $5,000 on average.

It is not possible to analyze precisely the full spillover impact of sub-prime foreclosures on African Americans, mainly because these data are not available yet. However, since these communities receive a disproportionate share of sub-prime home loans communities of color will be especially harmed. It was estimated that this lost home value translates into a decrease in the tax base, consumer expenditures, investment opportunities, and money circulating in communities of color. United for a Fair Economy estimates that borrowers or color have collectively lost between $164 billion and $213 billion in housing wealth as a result of sub-prime loans taken during the past eight years.

Whatever the exact figures, the bottom line is clear -- after centuries of being denied an opportunity to accumulate wealth, after a few decades of having limited opportunities, and after a generation during which African American families amassed significant wealth. The African American community now faces the greatest loss of financial wealth in its history. Institutional processes and racialized policy are trumping hard-earned educational, job, and income advances.

The Curse of Payday Lending

Payday lending primary loan process involves a lender providing a short-term unsecured loan to be repaid at the borrower's next payday. Verification of employment or income was required (via pay stubs and bank statements), although some payday lenders do not verify income or run credit checks. Individual companies and franchises have their respective underwriting criteria.

In the traditional retail model, borrowers visit a payday lending store and secure a small cash loan, with payment due in full at the borrower's next paycheck. The borrower writes a postdated check to the lender in the total amount of the credit plus fees. On the maturity date, the borrower is expected to return to the store to repay the loan in person. If the borrower does not repay the loan in person, the lender may redeem the check. If the account is short on funds to cover the check, the borrower may now face a bounced check fee from their bank in addition to the costs of the loan, and the loan may incur additional charges or an increased interest rate (or both) as a result of the failure to pay.

In the more recent innovation of online payday loans, consumers complete the loan application online (or in some instances via fax, especially where documentation is required). The funds are then transferred by direct deposit to the borrower's account, and the loan repayment or the finance charge was electronically withdrawn on the borrower's next payday.

User demographics

A family will use a payday loan if they are unbanked or underbanked, or lack access to a traditional bank account. The families profile of a payday loan user is disproportionately either of black or Hispanic descent, recent immigrants, or the under-educated. These individuals are least able to secure normal, lower-interest-rate forms of credit.

Since payday lending operations charge higher interest rates than traditional banks, they have the effect of depleting the assets of low-income communities. Most borrowers use payday loans to cover ordinary living expenses, not unexpected emergencies. The average borrower is indebted about five months of the year. Sadly, the simple solution for eliminating the need for Payday lending is community Credit Unions.

Summary

There was a determined effort since the end of slavery (1865) to destroy any effort of African Americans to build wealth. The end of slavery bought Black Codes, Peonage, Convict Leasing, Chain Gangs, finally the Ku- Kluck-Klan to maintain free labor for plantations.

The destruction Black Wall Street was the first of a series of economic plagues unleashed on Black wealth building in America at the end of slavery. Sadly, the end of Black Wall Street destroyed any example of a thriving community wealth building. It also clearly showed that there was no limit that whites would not go to destroy black wealth.

Sub-Prim, Redlining, and Pay- Day lending were the latest efforts at Black wealth destruction. Every effort was met with setbacks but not defeat. The Black economy (GDP) has continued to grow to(1.2) Trillion by 2018.

Credit Unions are the perfect solution for managing, growing, and protecting Black communities wealth. A credit Union provides every service that a community should ever need. The first and most important feature of a C.U. is, different from a commercial bank because it is federally regulated, community-owned, community staffed, yet service comparable to regular banks. Finally, a community CU prevents community "wealth predators."

CHAPTER 10

MAKE YOUR VOTE COUNT

In 2008 this country elected its first black president, Barak Obama; the response was the disastrous election of Donald Trump.

The history of black American's right to vote

1866: Civil Rights Act of 1866 grants citizenship, but not the right to vote, to all native-born Americans.

1869: Congress passed the 15th Amendment to the United States Constitution in 1869, which granted African-American men the right to vote by declaring the "right of citizens of the United States to vote shall not be denied or abridged by the United States or by any state on account of race, color, or previous condition of servitude."

At the time of its passage shortly after the Civil War, there was a huge debate between the suffragists, who wanted the right to vote for women and not for black men, at least not before them. Nonetheless, after the defeat of the Confederate Army, the Civil War Amendments (13th ending involuntary servitude except for the criminally convicted; the 14th guaranteeing due process and equal protection for all citizens, including recently emancipated black persons and the 15th

Amendment, ensuring the right to vote to black men) were passed by Congress.

On August 6, 1965, nearly 100 years after the Civil War, President Lyndon Johnson signed the Voting Rights Act into law. The voting rights law was the pinnacle of the Civil Rights Movement; it outlawed the discriminatory voting practices adopted in many southern states after the Civil War, including literacy tests and poll taxes as prerequisites to voting.

Its opponents have attacked it since it was enacted into law. This precious right, upon which the American democracy stands, has been a long and hard fight for black Americans and benefits all Americans. The road was long and hard.

Beginning in 1876, the Supreme Court presided over a three-decades-long dismantling of what seemed to be a constitutional guarantee of the right to vote for African-Americans. The groundwork was laid in May of that year, when, in *United States* v. *Reese*, the court determined that the 15th Amendment, which states that the right to vote "shall not be denied or abridged…on account of race, color, or previous condition of servitude," did not mean what it seemed to suggest.

As Justice Joseph Bradley wrote in a companion case, the amendment "confers no right to vote. That is the exclusive prerogative of the states. It does confer a right not to be excluded from voting because of race, color or previous condition of servitude, and this is all the right that Congress can enforce." Bradley thus transferred the burden of proof from the government that has denied someone's right to vote to the person whose rights had been rejected, a bar that would prove impossibly high.

In 1880, in a pair of cases decided the same day, the court overturned a West Virginia law that, by statute, limited jury service to white men, but sustained a murder conviction by an all-white jury in a Virginia case because, although no African-Americans were chosen to serve on juries, there was no specific law that prevented it. Southern whites got the idea. As long as a law did not announce its intention to discriminate, it would pass judicial muster.

When Justice Bradley, writing for an 8-1 majority in the Civil Rights Cases in 1883, declared the Civil Rights Act of 1875 unconstitutional and announced that black Americans would no longer be "the special favorite of the laws," white supremacists ramped up their efforts to keep black Americans from the ballot box, employing terror, fraud, and a series of ludicrous contrivances. The following are examples:

Violence

Violence was a principal means of direct disenfranchisement in the South before Redemption. In 1873, a band of whites murdered over 100 blacks who were assembled to defend Republican officeholders against attack in Colfax, Louisiana.

Fraud

Electoral fraud by ballot box stuffing, throwing out non-Democratic votes was the norm in the Southern states before legal means of dis-enfranchisement were entrenched. Between 1880 and 1901, Congress seated 26 Republican or Populist congressional candidates who had been "defeated" through electoral fraud.

Poll Taxes

Georgia initiated the poll tax in 1871 and made it cumulative in 1877 (requiring citizens to pay all back taxes before being permitted to vote). Every former Confederate state followed its lead by 1904. Although these taxes of $1-$2 per year may seem small, it was beyond the reach of many poor black and white sharecroppers, who rarely dealt in cash. The Georgia poll tax probably reduced overall turnout by 16-28%.

Literacy Tests

The first implicit literacy test was South Carolina's notorious "eight-box" ballot, adopted in 1882. Voters had to put ballots for separate offices in separate boxes. A ballot for the governor's race put in the box for the Senate seat would be thrown out. The order of the boxes was continuously shuffled, so that literate people could not assist illiterate voters by arranging their ballots in the proper order. The adoption of the secret ballot constituted another implicit literacy test since it prohibited anyone from assisting an illiterate voter in casting his vote. In 1890, Southern states began to adopt exact literacy tests to disenfranchise voters who also had a large differential racial impact, since 40-60% of blacks were illiterate, compared to 8-18% of whites. Poor, illiterate whites opposed the tests, realizing that they too would be disenfranchised. Southern states adopted an "understanding clause" or a "grandfather clause," which entitled voters who could not pass the literacy test to voting. The citizen had to demonstrate their understanding of the meaning of a passage in the constitution to the satisfaction of the registrar or was descended from someone eligible to vote in 1867, the year before blacks attained the franchise. Discriminatory administration ensured that blacks would not be likely to vote through the understanding clause. However, illiterate whites also felt the impact of the literacy tests, since some of the understanding and grandfather clauses expired after a few years, and some whites were reluctant to expose their illiteracy by publicly resorting to them.

Restrictive and Arbitrary Registration Practices

Southern states made registration difficult, by requiring frequent re-registration, long terms of residence in a district, registration at inconvenient times (e.g., planting season), provision of information unavailable to many blacks (e.g., street addresses, when black neighborhoods lacked street names and numbers), and so forth. When blacks managed to qualify for the vote even under these measures, registrars would use their discretion to deny them the vote anyway. Alabama's constitution of 1901 was explicitly designed to disenfranchise blacks by such restrictive and fraudulent means. Despite this, Jackson Giles, a black janitor, qualified for the vote under Alabama's constitution. He brought suit against Alabama on behalf of himself and 75,000 similarly qualified blacks who had been arbitrarily denied the right to register.

The White Primary

Disenfranchisement brought about one-party rule in the Southern states which meant that the Democratic nominee for any office was assured of victory in the general election guaranteeing the real electoral contest to the party primary. This fact provided yet another opportunity to disenfranchise blacks. Texas passed a law forbidding blacks from participating in Democratic primary elections.

Electoral College

Summary

"The 2012 turnout was a milestone for blacks and black politicians. "What it suggests is that there was an 'Obama effect' where people were motivated to support Barack Obama. But it also meant that black turnout may not always be high if future races aren't as salient especially for black voters."

Because of the Black population geographical distribution, the black voting population has an impact of (72) electoral college votes for president. Therefore, as was proven during the 2016 Trump/ Clinton election, a Democrat will always have a difficult time getting elected President without a high black turnout.

African Americans need to understand and appreciate their value in the electoral process.

The 2018 Georgia election shows that black voter suppression, a southern tradition, still flourishes.

Brian Kemp, candidate for governor in 2018, held two significant positions in Georgia politics, and he has been in the news for both of them. As the Republican nominee for governor, he was engaged in a fierce battle with Democrat Stacey Abrams, who, if she wins, would become the first female African-American governor in United States history. Polling indicates an extremely close race, one that could be decided by tens of thousands of votes.

Kemp was Georgia's current secretary of state, where one of his responsibilities is to oversee state elections. In that capacity, he had been engaged in a systematic campaign to restrict the number of Georgians allowed to cast ballots. In July 2017, Kemp's office purged nearly 600,000 people, or 8 percent of the state's registered voters, from the rolls; an estimated 107,000 were cut just because they hadn't voted in recent elections. Kemp blocked the registration of 53,000 state residents, 70 percent of whom were African-American and therefore could be reasonably expected to vote for Abrams. Both moves were entirely legal. Georgia, plus at least eight other states, has a "use it or lose" law that allows it to cancel voter registrations if the person hasn't voted in recent elections.

Georgia also has an "exact match" law, whereby a voter registration application must be identical to the information on file with Georgia's Department of Driver Services or the Social Security Administration. If they didn't match, or no such information is on record, then the registration was put on hold until the applicant can provide additional documents to prove their identity. The result was more than 50,000 applicants are on hold. (They can still vote, with a photo ID, but no doubt their pending status will discourage many.)

FINAL SUMMARY

True black history has been benchmarked by a series of social engineering events designed to diminish or destroy African American society. We are today, the product of political, social, and legal events at every turn.

Life under slavery was awful; Emancipation was supposed to eliminate those conditions. Emancipation gifted newly freed slaves with, the rebirth of white supremacy in the South which was accompanied by Black Codes, Chain Gangs, Peonage, Convict Leasing, and finally the Ku Klux Klan.

Out-migration from slavery should have been the beginning of a dream based on the initial success of Black Wall Street. Black Wall Street should have been used as the shining example going forward because it represented what Black community building success should look like.

Cabrini Greene, the end of the migration dream, represented the devastating effects of racial, social engineering. After the U.S. Supreme Court declared in 1888 racially based housing ordinances unconstitutional in 1917, segregation released the creative spirits of those who would oppress and dominate the weak and defenseless. Thus Cabrini Greene.

The Washington, D.C. public school system, before integration, was an example of a productive teaching/learning experience for black children. That system used the considerable advantage that segregation created; the highest educated black professionals had few opportunities for employment. Thus they turned to education. When school de-seg-regation started, the Black community focused only on college-level preparation, which ultimately lost most black students. Only (10% to 20%) of black kids desired to pursue a college education while forget-ting who wished to develop useful skills at the end of the high school tour. Those who drove the education agenda had two goals; integrate immediately, because "white schools were better," teach only academic skills because all black kids should be intellectuals, not service provid-ers. The result was a large portion of black students failed to meet minimum academic standards- they had little interest.

The Civil Rights Act of 1964 ended segregation in public places and banned employment discrimination by race, color, religion, sex or national origin, was considered to be one of the crowning legislative achievements of the civil rights movement. The truth was that the Civil Rights Act bought black America heroin, crack cocaine and the begin-ning of the end of intact black families as a method of undermining black completion. African Americans had become a society of drug addicts that continue to this day, ultimately preventing them from par-ticipating in developing wealth.

New York City's "man in the house rule" required welfare workers to make unannounced visits to determine if fathers were living in the home – if evidence of a male presence was found, cases were closed and welfare checks discontinued. Thus the beginning of the end of in-tact black families. Ronald Reagan's "Welfare Queen" narrative only reinforced existing white stereotypes about blacks.

The Nixon campaign in 1968 and the Nixon White House had two enemies: the anti-war left and black people. John Ehrlichman stated in a radio in-terview: *"We knew we couldn't make it illegal to be either against the war or blacks, but by getting the public to associate the hippies with marijuana and blacks with heroin, and then criminalizing both heavily, we could disrupt those communities."*

There was a media's portrayal of the African American community during the 1980s crack epidemic with countless stories of incurable "crack babies" who would inevitably grow up to be criminals. The "culture of poverty" welfare queens and poor people were themselves the cause of drug abuse, and the only solution to protect (white society) was swift, harsh and unrelenting punishment comprizing long jail sentences through the "War on Drugs."

There was a determined effort since the end of slavery (1865) to destroy any effort of African Americans to build wealth. The destruction Black Wall Street was the first of a series of economic plagues unleashed on Black wealth building in America at the end of slavery. Sadly, the end of Black Wall Street destroyed any example of a thriving black community wealth building. Sub-Prim, Redlining, and Pay- Day lending were the latest efforts at Black wealth destruction.

"The 2012 turnout was a milestone for blacks and black politicians. "What it suggests is that there was an 'Obama effect' where people were motivated to support Barack Obama. But it also meant that black turnout may not always be high if future races aren't as salient especially for black voters."

Because of the Black population geographical distribution, the black voting population has an impact of (72) electoral college votes for president. Therefore, as was proven during the 2016 Trump/ Clinton election, a Democrat will always have a difficult time getting elected President without a high black turnout.

African Americans need to understand and appreciate their value in the electoral process.

Index

CHAPTER I
PLANTATION SOCIAL DEVELOPMENT

1. African Roots Of African-American Culture. - Free Online .., https://www.thefreelibrary.com/African+roots+of+African-American+culture.-a05364 (accessed February 11, 2019).

2. Https://www.nps.gov/saga/learn/education/upload/African%20American%20History%20Timeline.pdf Website Title: African American History Timeline - National Park Service Date Accessed: January 04, 2019

3. Reconstruction - History, https://www.history.com/topics/american-civil-war/reconstruction (pg 8,9,10,11)(accessed January 29, 2019).

4. https://www.thoughtco.com/the-cotton-gin-in- Invention of the Cotton Gin and Its Historical Impact Date Accessed: January 04, 2019

5. Anita Johnson: The History Of Black-owned Banks, http://sacobserver.com/2016/02/anita-johnson-the-history-of-black-owned-banks/ (accessed February 21, 2019). (pg.117/118)

6. https://www.history.com/topics/black-history/underground-railroad Website Title: Underground Railroad - HISTORY Date Accessed: January 04, 2019

7. Slavery by Another Name History Background By Nancy O'Brien Wagner, Bluestem Heritage Group http://uccdarien. org/wp-content/uploads/2014/02/We-Are-One.pdf Website Title: We Are One Acts 2:1-11 - uccdarien.org Date Accessed: January 04, 2019

8. https://www.history.com/topics/black-history/underground-railroad Website Title: Underground Railroad – HISTORY Date Accessed: January 04, 2019

9. Website Title: Harriet Tubman – HISTORY Date Accessed: January 04, 2019

10. "Harriet Tubman Quotes." BrainyQuote.com. BrainyMedia Inc, 2019. 3 January 2019. https://www.brainyquote.com/quotes/harriet_tubman_310310

11. https://www.history.com/topics/black-history/underground-railroad Website Title: Underground Railroad - HISTORY Date Accessed: January 04, 2019

12. https://www.history.com/topics/american-civil-war/reconstruction Website Title: Reconstruction – HISTORY Date Accessed: January 04, 2019

13. https://www.history.com/topics/american-civil-war/black-leaders-during-reconstruction Website Title: Black Leaders During Reconstruction – HISTORY Date Accessed: January 04, 2019 (pg12,13,14)

14. http://bento.cdn.pbs.org/hostedbento- rod/filer_public/SBAN/Images/Classrooms/Slavery%20by%20Another%20Name%20History%20Background_Final.pdf Website Title: Slavery by Another Name History Background – PBS Date Accessed: January 04, 2019

15. Ukmix • View Topic - Black History Year https://www | Winner,. ukmix.org/forums/viewtopic.php?t=132432&start=150 (accessed January 29, 2019).

16. thoughtspoetryanything.blogspot.com/2012/ Website Title: Thoughts Poetry Anything: 2012 Date Accessed: January 04, 2019

17. http://bento.cdn.pbs.org/hostedbento- prod/filer_public/

SBAN/Images/Classrooms/Slavery%20by%20Another%20 Name%20History%20Background_Final.pdf

18. Website Title: Slavery by Another Name History Background – PBS Date Accessed: January 04, 2019

19. Slavery By Another Name - Giantdeadbody.com, https:// www.giantdeadbody.com/slavery-by-another-name (accessed February 06, 2019).

20. http://bento.cdn.pbs.org/hostedbento-   prod/filer_public/ SBAN/Images/Classrooms/Slavery%20by%20Another%20 Name%20History%20Background_Final.pdf

21. Website Title: Slavery by Another Name History Background – PBS Date Accessed: January 04, 2019

22. Website Title: Thoughts Poetry Anything: 2012 Date Accessed: January 04, 2019

23. Ford's Theatre Blog · Ford's Theatre, https://www.fords.org/ blog/post/how-to-write-an-essay-on-lincolns-assassination- (accessed January 25, 2019).

24. http://bento.cdn.pbs.org/hostedbento-   prod/filer_public/ SBAN/Images/Classrooms/Slavery%20by%20Another%20 Name%20History%20Background_Final.pdf

25. Website Title: Slavery by Another Name History Background – PBS Date Accessed: January 04, 2019 (pg.18/26)

26. Sharpe 2000 Ch 5 World War Ii Pp 116 148 33 Pages The .., https://www.coursehero.com/file/p68608u/Sharpe-2000- Ch-5-World-War-II-pp-116-148 (accessed January 21, 2019).

27. https://www.giantdeadbody.com/slavery-by-another-name

28. Slavery By Another Name History Background, https://bento. cdn.pbs.org/hostedbento-   prod/filer_public/SBAN/Images/ Classrooms/S (accessed January 29, 2019).

29. Website Title: Slavery By Another Name - giantdeadbody.com Date Accessed: January 04, 2019

30. thoughtspoetryanything.blogspot.com/2012/

31. Website Title: Thoughts Poetry Anything: 2012 Date Accessed: January 04, 2019

CHAPTER 2
POST CIVIL WAR (Lynch Time)

1. The Truth Behind '40 Acres And A Mule' | African American .., https://www.pbs.org/wnet/african-americans-many-rivers-to-cross/history/the-trut (accessed February 05, 2019).

2. https://www.history.com/topics/american-civil-war/black-leaders-during-reconstruction Website Title: Black Leaders During Reconstruction – HISTORY Date Accessed: January 05, 2019

3. The Historian Eric Foner introduced in his book, Reconstruction: America's Unfinished Revolution, 1863-1877

4. https://www.history.com/topics/american-civil-war/black-leaders-during-reconstruction Website Title: Black Leaders During Reconstruction – HISTORY Date Accessed: January 05, 2019

5. https://www.washingtonpost.com/news/retropolis/wp/2017/09/21/he-was-the-first-black-man-elected-to-congress-but-white-lawmakers-refused-to-seat-him/

6. Website Title: John Willis Menard: The first black man elected to Congress ... Date Accessed: January 05, 2019

7. U.s. Government Approval | 10 Outrageous Reasons Black .., https://3chicspolitico.com/2014/02/23/u-s-government-approval-10-outrageous-reas (accessed January 21, 2019).

8. https://www.washingtonpost.com/news/retropolis/wp/2017/09/21/he-was-the-first-black-man-elected-to-congress-but-white-lawmakers-refused-to-seat-him/ Website Title: John Willis

9. What Kinds Of Political Offices Did Blacks Hold After The .., https://classroom.synonym.com/kinds-political-offices-did-blacks-hold-after-civi (accessed February 05, 2019).

10. Menard: The first black man elected to ... Date Accessed: January 05, 2019

11. http://theweeklychallenger.com/he-was-the-first-black-man-elected-to-congress-but-white-lawmakers-refused-to-seat-him/

12. What Kinds Of Political Offices Did Blacks Hold After The .., https://classroom.synonym.com/kinds-political-offices-did-blacks-hold-after-civi (accessed January 29, 2019).

13. Website Title: He was the first black man elected to Congress. But white ...Date Accessed: January 05, 2019

14. https://www.history.com/topics/american-civil-war/black-leaders-during-reconstruction Website Title: Black Leaders During Reconstruction – HISTORY Date Accessed: January 05, 2019

15. http://www.memory.loc.gov/ammem/aaohtml/exhibit/aopart5b.html Website Title: African American Odyssey: Reconstruction and Its Aftermath ...Date Accessed: January 05, 2019

16. https://www.history.com/topics/american-civil-war/black-leaders-during-reconstruction Website Title: Black Leaders During Reconstruction – HISTORY Date Accessed: January 05, 2019

17. https://quizlet.com/261750066/crosby-flash-cards/ Website Title: Crosby Flashcards | Quizlet Date Accessed: January 05, 2019

18. https://www.britannica.com/topic/African-American/The-Civil-War-era Website Title: African Americans - The Civil War era | Britannica.com Date Accessed: January 05, 2019

19. https://www.u-s-history.com/pages/h411.html

20. Website Title: The Black Codes Date Accessed: January 05, 2019

21. https://www.u-s-history.com/pages/h411.html Website Title: The Black Codes Date Accessed: January 05, 2019

22. https://www.ajusd.org/Page/4492 Website Title: Miller, Jason / Reconstruction Date Accessed: January 05, 2019

23. https://www.coursehero.com/file/p3lfu02/Blacks-won-election-to-southern-state-governments-and-even-to-the-US-Congress/

24. Website Title: Blacks won election to southern state governments and even ..Date Accessed: January 05, 2019

25. https://www.naacp.org/history-of-lynchings/ Website Title:

NAACP | History of Lynchings Date Accessed: January 05, 2019
26. Wandrei, Kevin. "What Kinds of Political Offices Did Blacks Hold After the Civil War?" Synonym, https://classroom.synonym.com/kinds-political-offices-did-blacks-hold-after-civil-war-21046.html. Accessed 05 January 2019.
27. https://www.naacp.org/history-of-lynchings/ Naacp | History Of Lynchings (accessed January 05, 2019).
28. "10 Outrageous Reasons Black People Were Lynched In America." <https://atlantablackstar.com/2014/02/14/10-outrageous-reasons-black-people-were->.Web. 05 Jan. 2019
29. History Of Lynchings In America | Lipstick Alley, https://www.lipstickalley.com/threads/history-of-lynchings-in-america.102171/ (Date accessed January 05, 2019).
30. Fruits Of Reconstruction - The Library Of Congress, https://memory.loc.gov/ammem/aaohtml/exhibit/aopart5b.html (accessed March 02, 2019).

CHAPTER 3

1. POST WAR ECONOMIC DEVELOPMENT (End of Black Wall Street- Birth of the New Black Economy)
2. Great Migration - History, https://www.history.com/topics/black-history/great-migration (accessed January 20, 2019).
3. Ever Heard Of 'Black Wall Street'?
4. by Brandon Weber February 19, 2016 (accessed January 6, 2019)
5. Black Wall Street And The Destruction Of An Institution .., https://www.ebony.com/black- history/destruction-of-black-wall-street/ (accessed January 20, 2019).
6. Overview - Tulsa Historical Society - Smugmug, https://thsm.smugmug.com/Overview (accessed January 20, 2019).
7. Black Wall Street And The Destruction Of An Institution .., https://www.ebony.com/black-history/

destruction-of-black-wall-street/ (accessed January 21, 2019).

8. Panel Urges Oklahoma To Pay Reparations For 1921 Race Riot https://www.deseretnews.com/article/828381/Panel-urges-Oklahoma-to-pay-reparatio (accessed February 06, 2019).

9. 1921 Tulsa Race Riot – Aziz Bey Family Trust, https://northgate. network/2018/08/15/1921-tulsa-race-riot/ (accessed January 20, 2019).

10. Overview - Tulsa Historical Society - Smugmug, https://thsm. smugmug.com/Overview (accessed January 21, 2019).

11. The Trillion Dollar African American Consumer Market .., https://blackpast.org/perspectives/trillion-dollar-african-ameri-can-consumer-mar (accessed January 29, 2019

CHAPTER 4
SEGREGATION BY SOCIAL ENGINEERING

1. Chicago's Notorious Cabrini Green Housing Project- Whats .., https://www.youtube.com/watch?v=xTzVhwiaCww (accessed February 06, 2019).

2. Chicago: Cabrini-green 1942-2011 — Black Archives, http:// www.blvckvrchives.com/chicagocabrinigreen/ (accessed February 06, 2019).

3. Cabrini-green | Housing Development, Chicago, Illinois .., https://www.britannica.com/topic/Cabrini-Green (accessed February 06, 2019).

4. To What Extent Did The Establishment Of Cabrini Green.. https://answers.yahoo.com/question/index?qid= 20131228075756AAjaOir (accessed February 06, 2019).

5. Cabrini–green Homes - Wikipedia, https://en.wikipedia.org/ wiki/Cabrini%E2%80%93Green (accessed February 06, 2019).

6. https://www.history.com/topics/black-history/great-migration Access Date January 6, 2019

7. Publisher A&E Television Networks

8. Last Updated September 20, 2018

9. Original Published Date March 4, 2010 "African Americans." Encyclopedia.chicagohistory.org. Retrieved 23 September 2017.

10. "Archived copy." Archived from the original on 2007-09-27. Retrieved 2007-05-02.

11. Allen H. Spear, Black Chicago: The Making of a Negro Ghetto (1890-1920)

12. "Frommer's." Frommers.com. Retrieved 23 September 2017.

13. Nicholas Lemann, The Great Migration

14. Will Cooley, "Moving On Out: Black Pioneering in Chicago, 1915-1950," Journal of Urban History 36:4 (July 2010), 485-506.

15. "Housing and Race in Chicago." Chipublib.org. Retrieved 23 September 2017.

16. "Chicago: Destination for the Great Migration," The African-American Mosaic, Library of Congress.

17. Defender, Chicago (23 July 2010). "Chicago: Destination for the Great Migration - The African-American Mosaic Exhibition - Exhibitions (Library of Congress)." Loc.gov. Retrieved 23 September 2017.

18. Hirsch, Arnold Richard (1998). Making the Second Ghetto: Race and Housing in Chicago 1940-1960. Cabrini Green Housing Project, Chicago (1942 -2009) | The ..,

19. https://blackpast.org/aah/cabrini-green-housing-project-chicago-1942-2009 (accessed January 25, 2019, University of Chicago Press. ISBN 9780226342443.

20. "The Chicago's high murder rates drive an exodus of the black middle class." PBS Newshour. May 15, 2016. Retrieved on May 18, 2016.

21. "Westside Historical Society continues making history." Austinweeklynews.com. Retrieved 2016-10-1.

22. Cabrini–green Homes - Wikipedia, https://en.wikipedia.org/wiki/Cabrini%E2%80%93Green (accessed January 25, 2019).

23. History Of African Americans In Chicago - Wikipedia, https://en.wikipedia.org/wiki/Blacks_in_Chicago (accessed February

06, 2019).

24. Cabrini Green Housing Project, Chicago (1942 -2009) | The .., https://blackpast.org/aah/cabrini-green-housing-project-chicago-1942-2009 (accessed February 06, 2019).

Chapter 5
IMPACT OF BROWN V BOARD OF EDUCATION

1. Timeline » Tyler, Texas - History Of Racism & Hatred, http://www.tylerhistory.org/ (accessed February 06, 2019).

2. The enclosed pamphlet was developed in coordination with the Department of Education's Office of Postsecondary Education. Additional information on Executive Order 12677, Title 111, or programs on HBCUs, may be requested from the Assistant Secretary for Postsecondary Education, 400 Maryland Avenue, S. W., Washington, D.C. 20202.Date of Document 01/03/1991 (accessed January 25, 2019)

3. You Can't Fix What People Say The Best Thing To Do .., https://www.coursehero.com/file/prt2gt/You-cant-really-fix-what-people-say-the-b (accessed February 06, 2019).

4. Historically Black Colleges And Universities And Higher .., https://www2.ed.gov/about/offices/list/ocr/docs/hq9511.html (accessed January 25, 2019

5. Black Education /Schools: - Are HBCU'S Black Owned .., https://destee.com/threads/are-hbcus-black-owned.39539/ accessed January 25, 2019).

6. Morehouse College Spelman College And Tuskegee Institute .., https://www.coursehero.com/file/p7kdc0g/Morehouse-College-Spelman-College-and-Tu (accessed February 06, 2019).

7. Document Resume Ed 330 264 He 024 351 Title Historically .., https://files.eric.ed.gov/fulltext/ED330264.pdf (accessed January 25, 2019).

8. Historically Black Colleges And Universities And Higher .., https://www2.ed.gov/about/offices/list/ocr/docs/hq9511.html

(accessed January 25, 2019).

9. Black Education /Schools: - Are HBCUs Black Owned .., https://
destee.com/threads/are-hbcus-black-owned.39539/ (accessed
January 25, 2019).

10. Why Christians Should Celebrate Black History Month, http://
everysquareinch.net/why-christians-should-celebrate-black-
history-month/ (accessed March 02, 2019).

Chapter 6

1. DESTRUCTIVE EFFECTS OF CIVIL RIGHTS ACT OF 1964
Civil Rights Act Of 1875 - Wikipedia, ttps://en.wikipedia.org/
wiki/Civil_Rights_Act_of_1875 (accessed February 08, 2019).

2. A Fifty-Year March out of Poverty Authors Abigail Thernstrom,
Stephan Thernstrom Senior Fellow, Manhattan Institute

Chapter 7

1. WELFARE THE BEGINNING OF THE END OF INTACT
BLACK FAMILIES How racism shaped welfare policy in
America since 1935 Alma CartenAugust 22, 2016

2. Alma Carten, New York University Cammett, Ann. 2014.
"Deadbeat Dads & Welfare Queens: How Metaphor Shapes
Poverty Law." Boston College Journal of Law & Social Justice
34 (2): 233.

3. The Racist Roots Of Welfare Reform | The New Republic,
https://newrepublic.com/article/136200/racist-roots-welfare-
reform (accessed March 02, 2019).

Chapter 8

1. WAR ON DRUGS (Mass Incarceration of Black Males)
Nixon Aide Reportedly Admitted Drug War Was Meant To ..,
https://www.huffingtonpost.com/entry/nixon-drug-war-racist_
us_56f16a0ae4b03a640a (accessed February 25, 2019).

2. Detention Or Detox: Deconstructing America's New Face Of .., https://bpr.berkeley.edu/2017/01/23/detention-or-detox-de-constructing-americas-n (accessed March 02, 2019).

3. When Heroin Use Hit The Suburbs, Everything Changed - The .., https://www.washingtonpost.com/opinions/when-heroin-use-hit-the-suburbs-everythi (accessed January 25, 2019). (pg.110/112)

4. The Shame Is Not Ours: Black America, Poverty, And The War .., https://justicenotjails.org/black-america-drug-war/ (accessed February 06, 2019). (pg.102/103)

5. When A Drug Epidemic's Victims Are White - Vox, https://www.vox.com/identities/2017/4/4/15098746/opioid-heroin-epidemic-race (accessed February 22, 2019).

6. How The Opioid Epidemic Became America's Worst Drug Crisis .., https://www.vox.com/science-and-health/2017/3/23/14987892/opioid-heroin-epidemic (accessed February 22, 2019).

7. Crack, Heroin, And Race - The Atlantic, https://www.theatlantic.com/politics/archive/2015/08/crack-heroin-and-race/40101 (accessed February 23, 2019).

8. When heroin use hit the Suburbs By Stephen Lerner and Nelini Stamp May 16, 2014

9. Stephen Lerner is a fellow at Georgetown University's Kalmanovitz Initiative and the architect of the Justice for Janitors campaign. Nelini Stamp is the youth engagement director for Working Families.

Chapter 9
TRUE HISTORY OF ECONOMIC DEVELOPMENT (1 Trillion GPD Economy)

1. What Is Gross Domestic Product (GDP)? | Marginal .., https://www.mruniversity.com/courses/principles-economics-macro-economics/gross-d (accessed February 21, 2019).

2. Sub-prime As A Black Catastrophe - Prospect.org, HTTPs://prospect.org/article/sub-prime-black-catastrophe (accessed February 19, 2019). (pg. 122-135)

3. 5 Reasons Credit Unions Are Good For Your Community .., http://www.mcun.coop/credit-unions-community/ (accessed January 25, 2019).

4. Anita Johnson: The History Of Black-owned Banks, http://sacobserver.com/2016/02/anita-johnson-the-history-of-black-owned-banks/ (accessed January 29, 2019).

5. Redlining: Cfpb And Doj Action Require BancorpSouth Bank .., https://www.consumerfinance.gov/about-us/blog/redlining-cfpb-and-doj-action-requ (accessed February 22, 2019). (pg. 122\123)

6. Sub-prime As A Black Catastrophe - Prospect.org, https://prospect.org/article/sub-prime-black-catastrophe (accessed January 29, 2019).

7. Payday Loan - Wikipedia, https://en.wikipedia.org/wiki/Payday_loan (accessed February 22, 2019). (pg. 128/130)

Chapter 10
MAKE YOUR VOTE COUNT

1. The History Of Black American's Right To Vote, http://theweeklychallenger.com/the-history-of-black-americans-right-to-vote/ (accessed February 28, 2019).

2. America's Relentless Suppression Of Black Voters | The New .., https://newrepublic.com/article/151858/americas-relentless-suppression-black-vot (accessed February 28, 2019).

3. Techniques Of Direct Disenfranchisement, 1880-1965, http://www.umich.edu/~lawrace/disenfranchise1.htm (accessed February 28, 2019).

4. She was starting In 1877 When Georgia Passed The Cumulative Poll .., https://www.coursehero.com/file/p36gtks/Starting-in-1877-when-Georgia-passed-the (accessed February 28, 2019).

5. In 2012, Black Voter Turnout Surpassed White Turnout - CBS ..,
    https://www.cbsnews.com/news/in-2012-black-voter-turnout-
    surpassed-white-turnout (accessed March 04, 2019).

CPSIA information can be obtained
at www.ICGtesting.com
Printed in the USA
BVHW040951260419
546630BV00017B/340/P